THE WOR

THE AUTO

MARK R

WILLIAM HALE WHITE (1831–1913) was a
product of the strong Protestant tradition of
Bedford's Old Meeting, the chapel associated
with John Bunyan, but while studying for the
ministry in a Dissenting theological college, he
was expelled for heresy. He enjoyed a successful
career as a civil servant in the Admiralty; and in
his spare moments he produced a large volume
of journalism and six novels, of which *The
Autobiography of Mark Rutherford*, a fictionalized
account of his religious struggles, was the first.

WILLIAM S. PETERSON, Professor of English at
the University of Maryland, is the author and
editor of several books about Victorian literature
and is the editor of the quarterly journal *Papers
of the Bibliographical Society of America*.

THE WORLD'S CLASSICS

The Autobiography of Mark Rutherford
Dissenting Minister

Edited by his Friend
Reuben Shapcott

Edited with an Introduction by
WILLIAM S. PETERSON

Oxford New York
OXFORD UNIVERSITY PRESS
1990

Oxford University Press, Walton Street, Oxford OX2 6DP

Oxford New York Toronto
Delhi Bombay Calcutta Madras Karachi
Petaling Jaya Singapore Hong Kong Tokyo
Nairobi Dar es Salaam Cape Town
Melbourne Auckland

and associated companies in
Berlin Ibadan

Oxford is a trade mark of Oxford University Press

Introduction, Note on the Text, Select Bibliography,
Chronology, and Explanatory Notes © William S. Peterson 1990

First published by Oxford University Press 1936
First issued as a World's Classics paperback 1990

British Library Cataloguing in Publication Data
Rutherford, Mark, 1831–1913
The autobiography of Mark Rutherford, dissenting minister.
– (The world's classics).
I. Title II. Peterson, William S. (William Samuel), 1939–
823.8
ISBN 0-19-282594-1

Library of Congress Cataloging in Publication Data
White, William Hale, 1831–1913.
The autobiography of Mark Rutherford: dissenting minister/
edited by his friend Reuben Shapcott; edited with an introduction
by William S. Peterson.
p.   cm.—(The World's classics)
Includes bibliographical references.
Partial Contents: Partial contents: the autobiography of
Mark Rutherford—Notes on the book of Job—Principles—A mysterious
portrait.
I. Peterson, William S.   II. Title.   III. Series.
PR5795.W7A95   1990   823'.8—dc20   90-6989
ISBN 0-19-282594-1

Printed in Great Britain by
BPCC Hazell Books Ltd.
Aylesbury, Bucks

CONTENTS

INTRODUCTION

Writing in *Macmillan's Magazine* in March 1885, Mrs Humphry Ward observed: 'As a nation we are not fond of direct "confessions". All our autobiographical literature, compared to the French or German, has a touch of dryness and reserve. It is in books like *Sartor Resartus* or *The Nemesis of Faith*, *Alton Locke*, or *Marius [the Epicurean]*, rather than in the avowed specimens of self-revelation which the time has produced that the future student of the nineteenth century will have to look for what is deepest, most intimate, and most real in its personal experience.' This is an astute analysis of how the confessional impulse manifested itself in English literature during the nineteenth century, and Mrs Ward, a few years later, would have been able to add her own novel *Robert Elsmere* (1888) to a list of spiritual autobiographies cast in fictional form.

The niece of Matthew Arnold and a formidable bluestocking, Mrs Ward lived at the centre of English intellectual life in Oxford and London; she dined with the great men of the age, lectured and wrote on weighty subjects, and recorded in *Robert Elsmere* the anxiety felt by many Victorian intellectuals who had lost faith in the old religious verities. Yet even after rejecting orthodoxy, she remained at least obliquely identified with the Anglican establishment, for she was a regular church-goer until the end of her life and never wholly abandoned the hope that the Church of England might be reformed from within by pious sceptics such as herself. Like her more famous uncle, Mrs Ward wished to retain the ethos and some of the outward forms (especially the liturgy) of Anglicanism, while proclaiming at the same time that its dogmatic foundations were eroded. Despite the spiritual anguish of Robert Elsmere, we are uncomfortably aware of a certain cosiness pervading Mrs Ward's landscape; even as he is experiencing his dark night of the soul, Elsmere retains an unshakeable confidence in the traditional moral values of Christianity (if not its dogmas) and in his social position in the hierarchical world of late Victorian England. No longer an Anglican clergyman, he is nevertheless a Christian gentleman who has merely discarded a few clauses of the Nicene Creed.

But when we turn to the novels of Mrs Ward's contemporary, 'Mark Rutherford' (the pseudonym of William Hale White), we find ourselves suddenly moving across a bleaker, chillier terrain. It is true that literary historians have sometimes grouped together Mrs Ward and White as authors of two of the most notorious Victorian novels about the loss of religious faith; but this surely demonstrates how inadequate such simple categories are. Whereas Mrs Ward's writings reveal a complex Arnoldian distrust of traditional Christianity coupled with an awareness of its emotional and aesthetic appeal, White is the product of a stern Calvinistic passion for truth that had little patience for the seductive liturgical adornments that drew the Arnolds unwillingly back to the Church of England. If Robert Elsmere represents a nostalgia for the beauty and intellectual coherence of Christianity, Mark Rutherford embodies a more austere Puritan tradition that, in English literature at any rate, has its roots in the writings of John Bunyan.

The Autobiography of Mark Rutherford, published in 1881, is the first of White's six novels and the most directly confessional in nature. Supposedly edited after Rutherford's death by his friend Reuben Shapcott, it tells the story of a young man who is (in Arnold's inevitable phrase) caught between two worlds: having cast aside the older forms of belief, Rutherford finds himself shivering, defenceless, stripped naked of all spiritual armour, in an unbelieving world. Rutherford's tragedy is that he belongs to neither the desiccated Calvinism of Water Lane nor the equally dreary atheism of Wollaston's book shop in London. White had himself experienced that loss of community which he describes so eloquently in this novel. 'Now, although many of us may more or less widely have separated ourselves from the Christianity of the day, Christianity in a way is in our blood and all our thoughts are coloured by it,' he remarked in 1893. 'We cannot, or at least I cannot, come very near to a person to whom the Bible is nothing whatever. . . .'[1] The collapse of belief has created a God-shaped hole in Rutherford's heart, and the various desperate expedients to which he is driven in the novel—his short-lived decision to become a Unitarian minister, his Carlylean confidence in hard work as a means of stilling the questions in his mind, his Wordsworthian nature-worship—all represent attempts to fill that void.

From an historical point of view, the great achievement of *The Autobiography of Mark Rutherford* lies in its lifelike portrayal of English Dissenting life in a provincial town. White knew that life from the inside. There were of

[1] *Letters to Three Friends*, p. 146.

course other observers in the nineteenth century who were able to testify to the stultifying narrowness of such an existence. Matthew Arnold, who as an inspector of schools must have had many unhappy encounters with Dissenters, provided a series of vignettes in *Culture and Anarchy* (1869), of which perhaps the most memorable was this sentence in the chapter entitled 'Sweetness and Light': 'Look at the life imaged in such a newspaper as the *Nonconformist*—a life of jealousy of the Establishment, disputes, tea-meetings, openings of chapels, sermons; and then think of it as an ideal of a human life completing itself on all sides, and aspiring with all its organs after sweetness, light, and perfection!'

The substance of that accusation, it must be said, is not fundamentally different from Rutherford's description of his childhood and the experiences at Water Lane in the early chapters of the *Autobiography*. What irritated White about Arnold's treatment of Dissent, however, was his patronizing tone and his refusal to take the religious aspirations of the chapel seriously; offended by ugliness and parochialism, Arnold failed to see the heroic spiritual ideals that lay behind the decadent forms of nineteenth-century Calvinism. Arnold, characteristically, regretted that the small tradesmen of this world had not had the benefit of an Oxford education. White regretted that they no longer possessed the primitive zeal of Bunyan.

The creator of Mark Rutherford enjoyed the advantage of not only a sympathetic and intimate view of Victorian Protestantism but also a keen eye for detail, and it is this sensitivity of observation that makes the *Autobiography* more than merely a useful document of social history.

The portrait of Mr Snale, for example, is one of the best things of its kind in English literature: the force of White's satire upon religious hypocrisy belies the common complaint that he has no sense of humour, and it casts into the shade the rather feeble attempts by contemporaries like Dickens and Thackeray to make fun of pious Dissenters. Consider, for example, Rutherford's description of the Snales' drawing-room (pp. 33 4), which is a small masterpiece of symbolic rendering. The room contains four pictures. The first is a painting of Snale himself, his 'simper being preserved'. The equally repellent Mrs Snale is represented by a painting in which 'the peculiarly hard, heavy sensuality of the eye' is caught; she was, Rutherford adds, 'cruel, not with the ferocity of a tiger, but with the dull insensibility of a cartwheel, which will roll over a man's neck as easily as over a flint'. The two remaining pictures offer visual renditions of common Protestant themes: the descent of the Holy Ghost and the Second Coming of Christ. Both supply an ironic comment on the need for inner renewal which Christianity has rightly regarded as central to human experience. The Snales, despite their religious pretensions, are only too plainly imprisoned in unregenerate selves that have never been touched by the transforming experience of Pentecost.

The great ideas of Christianity have become crude daubs of paint on the Snales' drawing-room walls. When Rutherford visits the home of Edward Gibbon Mardon, he sees, by contrast, dignified portraits of Voltaire and Bacon—and, somewhat unexpectedly, a print of Dürer's St Jerome. As this detail suggests, Mardon is far from a conventional village atheist, and Rutherford finds in his household evidence of a spiritual and intellectual vitality that has departed from the world of the chapel-goers. Rutherford's gradual discovery about Christianity is not that it is untrue; like George Eliot, Arnold, Carlyle, and many other honest doubters, he remains convinced that the older faith had understood the essential verities of human existence. Instead he realizes that a particular variety of religious experience, conditioned by the historical forces of earlier centuries, had by his own day become a dead shell. As Carlyle had argued in *Sartor Resartus* (1834), the spiritual essence of Christianity was as real and vital as ever, but the tattered rags of dogma and pseudo-science that covered it would have to be discarded.

The structure of *The Autobiography of Mark Rutherford*, which appears deceptively linear, is in fact built around a series of contrasts between the false and the true. The most important incident in his adolescence, for instance, is his supposed conversion and formal profession of faith (pp. 10–12). Protestant believers often assumed that St Paul's dramatic conversion on the road to Damascus represented the normal pattern of entry into the faith, with the result that intense pressure was placed upon the young to follow his example by providing an emotional testimony of their spiritual transformation. As usual, Rutherford does not deny the kernel of truth that lies behind the practice (genuine conversion, he says, 'was occasionally a reality'), but he sees in this preoccupation with a public declaration of belief a symptom of degeneracy. Once the life has departed from a form, it is capable of producing only hypocrisy.

Yet Rutherford does, a little later, experience a

genuine conversion, and it is significant that when it comes, it takes place outside the framework of Christianity. Here at last is an undeniable spiritual rebirth (of the sort so grossly caricatured in the Snales' pictures); and we should not be surprised that in describing it, Rutherford instinctively invokes the Pauline precedent:

But one day in my third year [at a theological college], a day I remember as well as Paul must have remembered afterwards the day on which he went to Damascus, I happened to find amongst a parcel of books a volume of poems in paper boards. It was called 'Lyrical Ballads,' and I read first one and then the whole book. It conveyed to me no new doctrine, and yet the change it wrought in me could only be compared with that which is said to have been wrought on Paul himself by the Divine apparition. Looking over the 'Lyrical Ballads' again, as I have looked over it a dozen times since then, I can hardly see what it was which stirred me so powerfully, nor do I believe that it communicated much to me which could be put in words. But it excited a movement and a growth which went on till, by degrees, all the systems which enveloped me like a body gradually decayed from me and fell into nothing. (pp. 21–2)

The experience of reading Wordsworth creates in Rutherford that authentic process of renewal which is at the core of Christianity, yet paradoxically it is precisely this rebirth which makes him unfit to be a Dissenting minister. Having undergone the second birth recommended in the New Testament, he is regarded as a heretic by his congregation when he tries to breathe new life into the dead bones of their faith.

There is something so painful and outrageous about this that it borders on the amusing: White's straight-faced narrative here ought to remind us of Carlyle, who was capable of creating the same effect of grim humour through grotesque exaggeration. The *Autobiography* plainly owes a great deal to Carlyle, whom he described as 'the voice which in our century came from the deepest depths. In nobody do I find the immovable rock as I find it·in him.'[2] Like Carlyle, White struggled with the artistic problem of making the case for Christianity's fundamental truth while rejecting most of its formal creeds, and as in *Sartor Resartus* this typically Victorian argument was to be embodied in fictional form—as a parable, so to speak, that Christ might have told in the nineteenth century about how difficult it still was to find the straight and narrow path to heaven. In *Sartor Resartus* Carlyle had concealed the painful immediacy of his story by hiding behind two narrators, neither of whom bore his name. White was, if anything, even more self-effacing: not only did he provide himself with a Carlylean double layer of narrators but he declined to allow his name to appear on the title-page of any of his novels and hid his authorship of them even from close friends and family members.

The other writer with whom White displays obvious affinities is Bunyan, whose *Grace Abounding to the Chief of Sinners*, he said, 'is a terrible story of the mental struggle of a man of genius of a peculiarly nervous and almost hypochondriacal temperament; whose sufferings, although they are intertwisted with Puritanism, have roots which lie deep in our common nature'.[3] Except for the phrase 'of genius', that would serve very nicely as a summary of the *Autobiography* as well, and White undoubtedly saw in Bunyan a spiritual forebear and a

---

[2] *Letters to Three Friends*, p. 107.
[3] White, *John Bunyan*, p. 9.

model of prose style. Yet in reading the *Autobiography* one is always conscious of the considerable differences between Bunyan's Christian and the much more troubled and confused pilgrim who stumbles through White's novel. In this latter-day version of *The Pilgrim's Progress*, the protagonist inexplicably sets out in the wrong direction by journeying towards the City of Destruction as symbolized by dirty, crowded, spiritually empty London. From Stoke Newington, a village rapidly becoming an ugly suburb of the metropolis, the light of London seems to Rutherford 'like some unnatural dawn' (p. 123), a phrase which achieves its full effect only when we recall the religious rhapsodies inspired by real sunrises elsewhere in the novel. Once again we are invited to reflect upon the contrast between the true and the false.

It is at Stoke Newington that Rutherford's increasing melancholy is transformed into a black vision of despondency, and this serves as another reminder of the distance between Bunyan's pilgrim and White's. Rutherford, unlike his predecessor, never completely escapes the Slough of Despond and remains a prisoner of the Giant Despair almost to the end of his life. Rutherford's depression (to use a word more in fashion in our century) is in some respects the most profound mystery of this book. What is its source? In a letter written in 1882, White refers to Rutherford as a 'victim of the century',[4] and there can be no doubt that the author wishes us to see Rutherford's despair as a characteristic result of the collapse of religious orthodoxy in Victorian England.

[4] Irvin Stock, *Mark Rutherford (William Hale White): A Critical Study*, p. 80.

Nevertheless, White's phrase strikes one as slightly glib, perhaps even evasive, for every reader of the *Autobiography* must sense that though Rutherford's dark mood is meant to symbolize a collective loss of faith, it must have a private source as well. That suspicion is well founded. In some notes on his father by White's second son,[5] he acknowledges that the prolonged illness of his mother must have played a role:

The spectacle of her ever failing vitality, and my father's powerlessness to prevent it, afflicted him, as was natural, profoundly, and played a great part in deepening the melancholy which was the cross he carried with him through life. . . . The melancholy of which I speak and which was such a pronounced feature of my father's life, had other causes. He himself attributed it principally to incurable dyspepsia producing insomnia with all its train of evils. It is certain that it did spring largely from such troubles, but no reader of the 'Autobiography of Mark Rutherford' can, I think, fail to realize that it had other roots as well: in the unsolved problems of the age; the decay of religious faith; the ugliness of the industrial development; the terrible contrast of poverty and riches. It was a symptom of the age. My father had not the rich genius of such men as Carlyle and Ruskin, but he was of their epoch and their school, suffered as they, and showed the same unswerving refusal to compromise.

This testimony from the family compels us to face one of the more perplexing issues raised by a book like *The Autobiography of Mark Rutherford*: to what extent can it be regarded as a 'real' novel if it consists mainly of thinly concealed autobiography? Every work of fiction, needless to say, has embedded in it at least a few bits and pieces

[5] Bodleian Library MS Eng. misc. c. 445.

from the author's life, and even some very distinguished
novels appear to be largely the product of an imaginative
reshaping of actual events and persons. What seems to
put White's work in a different category, however, is our
awareness that he distrusted the human imagination and
sought to narrate the story of his pilgrimage as plainly
and directly as he could. That is not to say that the
outward circumstances of White's life and Rutherford's
were identical. William Hale White, unlike his fictional
counterpart, never became a clergyman because he was
expelled from a Dissenting college in London for holding
heretical views on the inspiration of the Bible, and
whereas Rutherford suffers in isolation, White's expulsion
drew a pamphlet from his father, a devout and en-
lightened man, and support from well-known Anglican
liberals such as F. D. Maurice and Charles Kingsley.
Young White became temporarily a public hero in the
cause of freedom of religious expression. Later he settled
into a solid career as a civil servant in the Admiralty,
married and raised a family, and in his final years
enjoyed a rapturously happy second marriage. Though
never part of the London literary intelligentsia, he met
and corresponded with many of the most famous writers
of the day, including Carlyle, Browning, and William
Morris. Even in old age he exhibited a lively interest in
literature and ideas.

This may surprise us if we have assumed that Mark
Rutherford's creator plodded morosely through life, cut
off from religion and society alike. The correspondences,
not surprisingly, exist at a deeper level. As Mrs Ward
remarked, the most striking self-revelations of the nineteenth century are to be found in fictional guise; *The*

Autobiography of Mark Rutherford, though it departs in many respects from the known facts of the novelist's life, offers us a compelling personal account of what it meant to be spiritually adrift in England a hundred years ago. It is an unhappy story that William Hale White chooses to tell, but he tells it with admirable skill, and readers may find some comfort in the final pages of the sequel, *Mark Rutherford's Deliverance* (1885), when this strangely brooding protagonist, shortly before his death, experiences a joyous epiphany on a holiday visit to the downs. White, as a good Wordsworthian, was aware of the full implications of the word *joy*. He makes it unmistakably clear that Mark Rutherford is in his last hours of life truly delivered from the burden of alienation from God and self.

A NOTE ON THE TEXT

William Hale White's first novel was published pseudonymously under the title *The Autobiography of Mark Rutherford, Dissenting Minister, Edited by His Friend, Reuben Shapcott* by Trübner in 1881. According to Simon Nowell-Smith, 200 copies bound in blue-green paper boards were issued on 4 March 1881 at five shillings. The rest of the edition of 500 copies was later bound in blue-black cloth with green endpapers and was sold for the same price.

In January 1885 Trübner issued a sequel, *Mark Rutherford's Deliverance: Being the Second Part of his Autobiography. Edited by his Friend, Reuben Shapcott*. A second edition of both novels appeared in a single volume in 1888, *The Autobiography of Mark Rutherford and Mark Rutherford's Deliverance. Edited by his Friend, Reuben Shapcott*, described on the title-page as 'Corrected and with Additions'. The corrections were minor, mainly revisions of punctuation, though they required a resetting of the type; White also added a new preface and 'A Mysterious Portrait', a short story now attributed to Rutherford which had first been printed anonymously in the *Birmingham Post*, 24 December 1881. Two essays appended to the book—'Notes on the Book of Job' and 'Principles'—had appeared earlier in the first edition of the *Deliverance*. The *Autobiography* and the *Deliverance* continued to be reprinted together for several decades thereafter, but there is no evidence that White had any role in altering the text of later impressions or editions.

Fascimile reprints of the first and second editions of the *Autobiography* have been published by Garland Publishers (1976) and Leicester University Press (1969) respectively. The present reprint is a reproduction of the text of the Oxford University Press edition (1936), which in turn is based on that of the second edition. The two essays and short story are reproduced from the OUP edition of the *Deliverance* (1936).

SELECT BIBLIOGRAPHY

William Hale White's six novels—*The Autobiography of Mark Rutherford* (1881), *Mark Rutherford's Deliverance* (1885), *The Revolution in Tanner's Lane* (1887), *Miriam's Schooling* (1890), *Catharine Furze* (2 vols., 1893), and *Clara Hopgood* (1896)— were issued in uniform editions by T. Fisher Unwin in 1905 and by the Oxford University Press in 1936. A useful 'Memorial Introduction' by H. W. Massingham (reprinted from the third edition of the *Autobiography*, 1923) appears in the latter.

Among the miscellaneous non-fictional works which he wrote, translated, or edited are *An Argument for an Extension of the Franchise* (1866), Spinoza's *Ethic* (translation, 1883) and *Tractatus de Intellectus Emendatione* (translation, 1895), *A Description of the Wordsworth and Coleridge Manuscripts in the Possession of Mr T. Norton Longman* (1897), *An Examination of the Charge of Apostasy against Wordsworth* (1898), *Coleridge's Poems: A Facsimile Reproduction of the Proofs and MSS. of Some of the Poems* (1899, with preface and notes by White), *John Bunyan* (biography, 1905), *Selections from Dr. Johnson's 'Rambler'* (1907), and Thomas Carlyle's *The Life of John Sterling* (1907).

His extensive contributions to periodicals have never been collected or even fully identified, though Merton, Stock, and Stone (see below) provide partial lists, and some of them were published in *Pages from a Journal* (1900; enlarged second edition, 1910), *More Pages from a Journal* (1910), and *Last Pages from a Journal* (1915).

The most authoritative account of his life is Catherine Macdonald Maclean's *Mark Rutherford: A Biography of*

William Hale White (1955), which may be supplemented
with William Robertson Nicoll's *Memories of Mark Rutherford*
(1924), Hans Klinke's *William Hale White, Versuch einer
Biographie* (1930), and Wilfred Stone's book (see below).
There is much material about the final years in Sussex in
The Groombridge Diary (1924) by Dorothy White, his second
wife. Selections from his correspondence are available in
Letters to Three Friends (1924), and some autobiographical
notes made by White for his children were published after
his death under the title *The Early Life of Mark Rutherford*
(1913).

The following are the major critical studies: Ursula
Buckmann, *William Hale White (Mark Rutherford) and the
Problem of Self-Adjustment in a World of Changing Values* (1950);
Wilfred H. Stone, *Religion and Art of William Hale White
(Mark Rutherford)* (1954); Irvin Stock, *William Hale White
(Mark Rutherford): A Critical Study* (1956); Stephen Merton,
Mark Rutherford (William Hale White) (1967); and Catherine
R. Harland, *Mark Rutherford: The Mind and Art of William
Hale White* (1988). He has also been the subject of a number
of doctoral theses.

The best short analysis of White's temperament and
fiction is a chapter in Basil Willey's *More Nineteenth Century
Studies* (1956). Other useful brief discussions are to be found
in Massingham's 'Memorial Introduction' (cited above);
A. E. Taylor, 'The Novels of Mark Rutherford', *Essays and
Studies by Members of the English Association* (1914); Margaret
Maison, *Search Your Soul, Eustace: A Survey of the Religious
Novel in the Victorian Age* (1961); and John Lucas, *The
Literature of Change: Studies in the Nineteenth-Century Provincial
Novel* (second edition, 1980). Two studies which place
White's work in the broader context of English Non-
conformity are Valentine Cunningham, *Everywhere Spoken*

Against: Dissent in the Victorian Novel (1975), and Donald Davie, *A Gathered Church: The Literature of the English Dissenting Interest, 1700–1930* (1978).

The most comprehensive lists of works by and about White are in *The New Cambridge Bibliography of English Literature*; Simon Nowell-Smith, 'Mark Rutherford: A Short Bibliography of the First Editions', *Bookman's Journal* (supplement, 1930); W. Eugene Davis, 'William Hale White (Mark Rutherford): An Annotated Bibliography of Writings about Him', *English Literature in Transition* (1967); and the bibliographies in the books by Stock, Merton, Harland, and Stone.

There are important collections of White's papers in the University of British Columbia (the Colbeck Collection), the Bodleian Library, and the Bedford Public Library.

Quotes Passim in the *Thomas More*, *1750*, and *Dorothy Drew: A Chelsea Sketch: To Adelheid zu Ilm Leipsic: Thannelitz Infant, 1760, 1761 (?)*.

The great Compendium lists of works are and about White are in *The New Cambridge Bibliography of English Literature*, Sixth, Marx, Hartnoll, *A Short Bibliography of the First Editions*, *see below, Jones (supplement), *1906, J. W. Eugene Dietz, William Hale Young (1898, Ruppet); An *Annotated Bibliography of Writings about Him, 1944; Memoranda and outlines (1910), and the Bibliographies in the books by Stone, &c. See England, and Stone.

There are important collections of White's papers in the University of Virginia Colonial (the Colbeck Collection), the Kelland Library, and the Bodleian Public Library.

A CHRONOLOGY OF
WILLIAM HALE WHITE

1831   Born 22 December in Bedford, son of William
        and Mary White.

1840   Enters English School, Angel Street, Bedford.

1846   Leaves English School.

1848   February, admitted to membership in the Old
        Meeting (later known as the Bunyan Meeting),
        Bedford. Autumn, matriculates at Countess of
        Huntingdon's College, Cheshunt, Hertfordshire.

1851   October, transfers to New College, St John's Wood,
        London.

1852   17 March, expelled from New College with two other
        students for questioning the authority of the
        Scriptures. Autumn, appointed schoolmaster in Stoke
        Newington but abandons position within a day or
        two; begins working for John Chapman, publisher
        and bookseller, in London.

1854   February, leaves Chapman's; becomes a clerk in the
        Registrar-General's Office, Somerset House, London.

1855   January, White's parents move to London; father
        appointed Doorkeeper of the House of Commons.

1856   22 December, marries Harriet Arthur.

1857   12 March, becomes Registrar of Births and Deaths,
        Marylebone (but continues working at Somerset
        House). 7 November, first child, William Hale, born.

1858   December, appointed to clerkship in the Accountant-
        General's Department of the Admiralty. June–July,
        visits Germany.

1861   Summer, begins to write regularly for the *Aberdeen
        Herald* (until January 1872). 23 October, son John
        Harry born.

1897   31 May, *A Description of the Wordsworth and Coleridge Manuscripts in the Possession of Mr T. Norton Longman* published.

1898   28 February, *An Examination of the Charge of Apostasy against Wordsworth* published.

1899   8 May, moves to Crowborough, Tunbridge Wells. July, edition of *Coleridge's Poems: A Facsimile Reproduction of the Proofs and MSS. of Some of the Poems* published.

1900   December, *Pages from a Journal* published.

1903   14 June, moves to Groombridge, Sussex.

1904   October, *John Bunyan* published (dated 1905 on title-page).

1907   March, edition of *Selections from Dr. Johnson's 'Rambler'* published. 26 November, edition of Thomas Carlyle's *The Life of John Sterling* published.

1910   20 October, *More Pages from a Journal* published.

1911   8 April, marries Dorothy Horace Smith.

1913   14 March, dies at Groombridge. 24 July, *The Early Life of Mark Rutherford* published.

1915   8 July, *Last Pages from a Journal published.*

1924   1 May, *Letters to Three Friends* published.

The Autobiography of
Mark Rutherford

CONTENTS

PREFACE TO THE SECOND EDITION

THE present edition is a reprint of the first, with corrections of several mistakes which had been overlooked. It also contains in addition a short story 'A Mysterious Portrait' which, although it was written by my friend when he was young, seemed to me worth preserving.

There is one observation which I may perhaps be permitted to make on re-reading after some years this autobiography. Rutherford, at any rate in his earlier life, was an example of the danger and the folly of cultivating thoughts and reading books to which he was not equal, and which tend to make a man lonely.

It is all very well that remarkable persons should occupy themselves with exalted subjects, which are out of the ordinary road which ordinary humanity treads; but we who are not remarkable make a very great mistake if we have anything to do with them. If we wish to be happy, and have to live with average men and women, as most of us have to live, we must learn to take an interest in the topics which concern average men and women. We think too much of ourselves. We ought not to sacrifice a single moment's pleasure in our attempt to do something which is too big for us, and as a rule, men and women are always attempting what is too big for them. To ninety-nine young men out of a hundred, or perhaps ninety-nine thousand nine hundred and ninety-nine out of a hundred thousand, the wholesome healthy doctrine is, 'Don't bother yourselves with what is beyond you; try to lead a sweet, clean, wholesome life, keep yourselves in health above everything, stick to your work, and when your day is done amuse and refresh yourselves.' It is not only a duty to ourselves, but it is a duty to others to take this course. Great men do the world much good, but not without some harm, and we have no business to be troubling ourselves with their dreams if we have duties which lie nearer home amongst persons to whom these dreams are incomprehensible. Many a man goes into his study, shuts himself up with his poetry or his psychology, comes out, half understanding what he has read, is miserable because he cannot find anybody with whom he can talk about it, and misses altogether the far more genuine joy which he could have obtained from a game with his children, or listening to what his wife had to tell him about her neighbours.

'Lor, miss, you haven't looked at your new bonnet to-day,' said a servant-girl to her young mistress.

'No, why should I? I did not want to go out.'

'Oh, how can you? why, I get mine out and look at it every night.'

She was happy for a whole fortnight with a happiness cheap at a very high price.

That same young mistress was very caustic upon the women who block the pavement outside drapers' shops, but surely she was unjust. They always seem unconscious, to be enjoying themselves intensely and most innocently, more so probably than an audience at a Wagner concert. Many persons with refined minds are apt to depreciate happiness, especially if it is of 'a low type.' Broadly speaking, it is the one thing worth having, and low or high, if it does no mischief, is better than the most spiritual misery.

Metaphysics, and theology, including all speculations on the why and the wherefore, optimism, pessimism, freedom, necessity, causality, and so forth, are not only for the most part loss of time, but frequently ruinous. It is no answer to say that these things force themselves upon us, and that to every question we are bound to give or try to give an answer. It is true, although strange, that there are multitudes of burning questions which we must do our best to ignore, to forget their existence; and it is not more strange, after all, than many other facts in this wonderfully mysterious and defective existence of ours. One fourth of life is intelligible, the other three fourths is unintelligible darkness; and our earliest duty is to cultivate the habit of not looking round the corner.

'Go thy way, eat thy bread with joy, and drink thy wine with a merry heart; for God hath already accepted thy works. Let thy garments be always white, and let not thy head lack ointment. Live joyfully with the wife whom thou lovest all the days of the life of thy vanity, which He hath given thee under the sun, all the days of thy vanity: for that is thy portion in life.'*

R. S.

THIS is the night when I must die,
   And great Orion walketh high
In silent glory overhead:
He'll set just after I am dead.

A week this night, I'm in my grave:
Orion walketh o'er the wave:
Down in the dark damp earth I lie,
While he doth march in majesty.

A few weeks hence and spring will come;
The earth will bright array put on
Of daisy and of primrose bright,
And everything which loves the light.

And some one to my child will say,
'You'll soon forget that you could play
Beethoven; let us hear a strain
From that slow movement once again.'

And so she'll play that melody,
While I among the worms do lie;
Dead to them all, for ever dead;
The churchyard clay dense overhead.

I once did think there might be mine
One friendship perfect and divine;
Alas! that dream dissolved in tears
Before I'd counted twenty years.

For I was ever commonplace;
Of genius never had a trace;
My thoughts the world have never fed,
Mere echoes of the book last read.

Those whom I knew I cannot blame:
If they are cold, I am the same:
How could they ever show to me
More than a common courtesy?

There is no deed which I have done;
There is no love which I have won,
To make them for a moment grieve
That I this night their earth must leave.

Thus, moaning at the break of day,
A man upon his deathbed lay;
A moment more and all was still;
The Morning Star came o'er the hill.

But when the dawn lay on his face,
It kindled an immortal grace;
As if in death that Life were shown
Which lives not in the great alone.

Orion sank down in the west
Just as he sank into his rest;
I closed in solitude his eyes,
And watched him till the sun's uprise.

CHAPTER I

CHILDHOOD

Now that I have completed my autobiography up to the present year, I sometimes doubt whether it is right to publish it. Of what use is it, many persons will say, to present to the world what is mainly a record of weaknesses and failures? If I had any triumphs to tell; if I could show how I had risen superior to poverty and suffering; if, in short, I were a hero of any kind whatever, I might perhaps be justified in communicating my success to mankind, and stimulating them to do as I have done. But mine is the tale of a commonplace life, perplexed by many problems I have never solved; disturbed by many difficulties I have never surmounted; and blotted by ignoble concessions which are a constant regret. I have decided, however, to let the manuscript remain. I will not destroy it, although I will not take the responsibility of printing it. Somebody may think it worth preserving; and there are two reasons why they may think so, if there are no others. In the first place, it has some little historic value, for I feel increasingly that the race to which I belonged is fast passing away, and that the Dissenting minister of the present day is a different being altogether from the Dissenting minister of forty years ago. In the next place, I have observed that the mere knowing that other people have been tried as we have been tried is a consolation to us, and that we are relieved by the assurance that our sufferings are not special and peculiar, but common to us with many others. Death has always been a terror to me, and at times, nay generally, religion and philosophy have been altogether unavailing to mitigate the terror in any way. But it has been a comfort to me to reflect that whatever death may be, it is the inheritance of the whole human race; that I am not singled out, but shall merely have to pass through what the weakest have had to pass through before me. In the worst of maladies, worst at least to me, those which are hypochondriacal, the healing effect which is produced by the visit of a friend who can simply say, 'I have endured all that,' is most marked. So it is not impossible that some few whose experience has been like mine may, by my example, be freed from that sense of solitude which they find so depressing.

I was born, just before the Liverpool and Manchester Railway*was opened, in a small country town*in one of the Midland shires. It is now semi-manufacturing, at the junction of three or four lines of railway, with hardly a trace left of what it was fifty years ago. It then consisted of one long main street, with a few other streets branching from it at right angles. Through this street the mail-coach rattled at night, and the huge waggon rolled through it, drawn by four horses, which twice a week travelled to and from London and brought us what we wanted from the great and unknown city. My father and mother belonged to the ordinary English middle class of well-to-do shopkeepers. My mother's family came from a little distance, but my father's had lived in those parts for centuries. I remember perfectly well how business used to be carried on in those days. There was absolutely no competition, and although nobody in the town who was in trade got rich, except the banker and the brewer, nearly everybody was tolerably well off, and certainly not pressed with care as their successors are now. The draper, who lived a little way above us, was a deacon in our chapel, and every morning, soon after breakfast, he would start off for his walk of about four miles, stopping by the way to talk to his neighbours about the events of the day. At eleven o'clock or thereabouts, he would return and would begin work. Everybody took an hour for dinner—between one and two, and at that time, especially on a hot July afternoon, the High Street was empty from end to end and the profoundest peace reigned.

My life as a child falls into two portions, sharply divided,—week-day and Sunday. During the week-day I went to the public school, where I learned little or nothing that did me much good. The discipline of the school was admirable, and the headmaster was penetrated with a most lofty sense of duty, but the methods of teaching were

very imperfect. In Latin we had to learn the Eton
Latin Grammar*till we knew every word of it by
heart, but we did scarcely any retranslation from
English into Latin. Much of our time was wasted
on the merest trifles, such as learning to write, for
example, like copperplate, and, still more extraordinary, in copying the letters of the alphabet as
they are used in printing. But we had two half-
holidays in the week, which seem to me now to
have been the happiest part of my life. A river ran
through the town,* and on summer Wednesdays
and Saturdays we wandered along its banks for
miles, alternately fishing and bathing. I remember whole afternoons in June, July, and August,
passed half-naked or altogether naked in the solitary meadows and in the water; I remember the
tumbling weir with the deep pool at the bottom
in which we dived; I remember, too, the place
where we used to swim across the river with our
clothes on our heads, because there was no bridge
near, and the frequent disaster of a slip of the
braces in the middle of the water, so that shirt,
jacket, and trousers were soaked, and we had to
lie on the grass in the broiling sun without a rag
on us till everything was dry again. In winter our
joys were of a different kind, but none the less
delightful. If it was a frost, we had skating; not
like the skating on a London pond, but over long
reaches, and if the locks had not intervened, we
might have gone a day's journey on the ice without

a stoppage. If there was no ice we had football, and what was still better, we could get up a steeple-chase on foot straight across hedge and ditch. In after-years, when I lived in London, I came to know children who went to school in Gower Street, and travelled backwards and forwards by omnibus, children who had no other recreation than an oc-casional visit to the Zoological Gardens, or a some-what sombre walk up to Hampstead to see their aunt; and I have often regretted that they never had any experience of those perfect poetic pleasures which the boy enjoys whose childhood is spent in the country, and whose home is there. A country boarding-school is something altogether different. On the Sundays,*however, the compensation came. It was a season of unmixed gloom. My father and mother were rigid Calvinistic Independents,* and on that day no newspaper nor any book more secular than the Evangelical Magazine*was toler-ated. Every preparation for the Sabbath had been made on the Saturday, to avoid as much as possible any work. The meat was cooked beforehand, so that we never had a hot dinner even in the coldest weather; the only thing hot which was permitted was a boiled suet pudding, which cooked itself while we were at chapel, and some potatoes which were prepared after we came home. Not a letter was opened unless it was clearly evident that it was not on business, and for opening these an apology was always offered that it was possible they might contain some announcement of sickness. If on cursory inspection they appeared to be ordinary letters, although they might be from relations or friends, they were put away. After family prayer and breakfast the business of the day began with the Sunday-school at nine o'clock. We were taught our Catechism and Bible there till a quarter past ten. We were then marched across the road into the chapel,* a large old-fashioned building dating from the time of Charles II. The floor was covered with high pews. The roof was supported by three or four tall wooden pillars which ran from the ground to the ceiling, and the galleries by shorter pillars. There was a large oak pulpit on one side against the wall, and down below, immediately under the minister, was the 'singing pew,'*where the singers and musicians sat, the musicians being performers on the clarionet, flute, violin, and violoncello. Right in front was a long enclosure, called the communion pew, which was usually occupied by a number of the poorer members of the congregation. There were three services every Sunday, besides intermitting prayer-meetings, but these I did not as yet attend. Each service consisted of a hymn, reading the Bible, another hymn, a prayer, the sermon, a third hymn, and a short final prayer. The reading of the Bible was unaccompanied with any observations or explanations, and I do not remember that I ever once heard a mistranslation corrected. The first, or

long prayer, as it was called, was a horrible hypocrisy, and it was a sore tax on the preacher to
get through it. Anything more totally unlike the
model recommended to us in the New Testament
cannot well be imagined. It generally began with
a confession that we were all sinners, but no individual sins were ever confessed, and then ensued
a kind of dialogue with God, very much resembling
the speeches which in later years I have heard
in the House of Commons from the movers and
seconders of addresses to the Crown at the opening
of Parliament. In all the religion of that day
nothing was falser than the long prayer. Direct
appeal to God can only be justified when it is
passionate. To come maundering into His presence when we have nothing particular to say is
an insult, upon which we should never presume if
we had a petition to offer to any earthly personage.
We should not venture to take up his time with
commonplaces or platitudes; but our minister
seemed to consider that the Almighty, who had
the universe to govern, had more leisure at His
command than the idlest lounger at a club. Nobody ever listened to this performance. I was a
good child on the whole, but I am sure I did not;
and if the chapel were now in existence, there
might be traced on the flap of the pew in which we
sat, many curious designs due to these dreary per-
formances. The sermon was not much better. It
generally consisted of a text, which was a mere peg

for a discourse, that was pretty much the same from
January to December. The minister invariably
began with the fall of man; propounded the scheme
of redemption, and ended by depicting in the
morning the blessedness of the saints, and in the
evening the doom of the lost. There was a tradition
that in the morning there should be 'experience,'
that is to say, comfort for the elect, and that the
evening should be appropriated to their less for-
tunate brethren. The evening service was the
most trying to me of all these. I never could keep
awake, and knew that to sleep under the Gospel
was a sin. The chapel was lighted in winter by
immense chandeliers with tiers of candles all
round. These required perpetual snuffing, and
I can see the old man going round the chandeliers
in the middle of the service with a mighty pair of
snuffers which opened and shut with a loud click.
How I envied him because he had a semi-secular
occupation which prevented that terrible drowsiness! How I envied the pew-opener, who was
allowed to stand at the vestry door, and could slip
into the vestry every now and then, or even into
the burial-ground if he heard irreverent boys playing there! The atmosphere of the chapel on hot
nights was most foul, and this added to my dis-
comfort. Oftentimes in winter, when no doors or
windows were open, I have seen the glass panes
streaming with wet inside, and women carried out
fainting. On rare occasions I was allowed to go

with my father when he went into the villages to preach. As a deacon he was also a lay-preacher, and I had the ride in the gig out and home, and tea at a farmhouse. Perhaps I shall not have a better opportunity to say that, with all these drawbacks, my religious education did confer upon me some positive advantages. The first was a rigid regard for truthfulness. My parents never would endure a lie or the least equivocation. The second was purity of life, and I look upon this as a simply incalculable gain. Impurity was not an excusable weakness in the society in which I lived; it was a sin for which dreadful punishment was reserved. The reason for my virtue may have been a wrong reason, but anyhow I was saved, and being saved, much more was saved than health and peace of mind. To this day I do not know where to find a weapon strong enough to subdue the tendency to impurity in young men; and although I cannot tell them what I do not believe, I hanker sometimes after the old prohibitions and penalties. Physiological penalties are too remote, and the subtler penalties—the degradation, the growth of callousness to finer pleasures, the loss of sensitiveness to all that is most nobly attractive in woman —are too feeble to withstand temptation when it lies in ambush like a garrotter, and has the reason stunned in a moment. The only thing that can be done is to make the conscience of a boy generally tender, so that he shrinks instinctively from the monstrous injustice of contributing for the sake of his own pleasure to the ruin of another. As soon as manhood dawns, he must also have his attention absorbed on some object which will divert his thoughts intellectually or ideally, and by slight yet constant pressure, exercised not by fits and starts, but day after day, directly and indirectly, his father must form an antipathy in him to brutish selfish sensuality. Above all, there must be no toying with passion, and no books permitted, without condemnation and warning, which are not of a heroic turn. When the boy becomes a man he may read Byron without danger. To a youth he is fatal. Before leaving this subject I may observe, that parents greatly err by not telling their children a good many things which they ought to know. Had I been taught when I was young a few facts about myself, which I only learned accidentally long afterwards, a good deal of misery might have been spared me.

Nothing particular happened to me till I was about fourteen, when I was told it was time I became converted. Conversion, amongst the Independents and other Puritan sects, is supposed to be a kind of miracle wrought in the heart by the influence of the Holy Spirit, by which the man becomes something altogether different to what he was previously. It affects, or should affect, his character; that is to say, he ought after conversion to be better in every way than he was before: but this is not considered as its main consequence. In its essence it is a change in the emotions and increased vividness of belief. It is now altogether untrue. Yet it is an undoubted fact that in earlier days, and, indeed, in rare cases, as late as the time of my childhood, it was occasionally a reality. It is possible to imagine that under the preaching of Paul sudden conviction of a life misspent may have been produced with sudden personal attachment to the Galilean who, until then, had been despised. There may have been prompt release of unsuspected powers, and as prompt an imprisonment for ever of meaner weaknesses and tendencies; the result being literally a putting off of the old, and a putting on of the new man. Love has always been potent to produce such a transformation, and the exact counterpart of conversion, as it was understood by the apostles, may be seen whenever a man is redeemed from vice by attachment to some woman whom he worships, or when a girl is reclaimed from idleness and vanity by becoming a mother. But conversion, as it was understood by me and as it is now understood, is altogether unmeaning. I knew that I had to be 'a child of God,' and after a time professed myself to be one, but I cannot call to mind that I was anything else than I always had been, save that I was perhaps a little more hypocritical; not in the sense that I professed to others what I knew I did not believe, but in the sense that I professed it to myself. I was obliged

to declare myself convinced of sin; convinced of
the efficacy of the atonement; convinced that I
was forgiven; convinced that the Holy Ghost was
shed abroad in my heart; and convinced of a great
many other things which were the merest phrases.
However, the end of it was, that I was proposed
for acceptance, and two deacons were deputed, in
accordance with the usual custom, to wait upon
me and ascertain my fitness for membership. What
they said and what I said has now altogether
vanished; but I remember with perfect distinctness the day on which I was admitted. It was the
custom to demand of each candidate a statement
of his or her experience. I had no experience to
give;*and I was excused on the grounds that I had
been the child of pious parents, and consequently
had not undergone that convulsion which those,
not favoured like myself, necessarily underwent
when they were called. I was now expected to
attend all those extra services which were specially
for the church. I stayed to the late prayer-meeting
on Sunday; I went to the prayer-meeting on week-
days, and also to private prayer-meetings. These
services were not interesting to me for their own
sake. I thought they were, but what I really liked
was clanship and the satisfaction of belonging to
a society marked off from the great world. It
must also be added that the evening meetings
afforded us many opportunities for walking home
with certain young women, who, I am sorry to

say, were a more powerful attraction, not to me only but to others, than the prospect of hearing brother Holderness, the travelling draper, confess crimes which, to say the truth, although they were many according to his own account, were never given in that detail which would have made his confession of some value. He never prayed without telling all of us that there was no health in him, and that his soul was a mass of putrefying sores; but everybody thought the better of him for his self-humiliation. One actual indiscretion, however, brought home to him would have been visited by suspension or expulsion.

CHAPTER II

PREPARATION

IT was necessary that an occupation should be found for me, and after much deliberation it was settled that I should 'go into the ministry.' I had joined the church, I had 'engaged in prayer' publicly, and although I had not set up for being extraordinarily pious, I was thought to be as good as most of the young men who professed to have a mission to regenerate mankind. Accordingly, after some months of preparation, I was taken to a Dissenting College*not very far from where we lived. It was a large old-fashioned house with a newer building annexed, and was surrounded with a garden and with meadows. Each student had a separate room, and all had their meals together in a common hall. Altogether there were about forty of us. The establishment consisted of a President, an elderly gentleman who had an American degree of doctor of divinity, and who taught the various branches of theology. He was assisted by three professors, who imparted to us as much Greek, Latin, and mathematics as it was considered that we ought to know. Behold me, then, beginning a course of training which was to prepare me to meet the doubts of the nineteenth century; to be the guide of men; to advise them in their perplexities; to suppress their tempestuous lusts; to lift them above their petty cares, and to lead them heavenward! About the Greek and Latin and the secular part of the college discipline I will say nothing, except that it was generally inefficient. The theological and biblical teaching was a sham. We had come to the college in the first place to learn the Bible. Our whole existence was in future to be based upon that book; our lives were to be passed in preaching it. I will venture to say that there was no book less understood either by students or professors. The President had a course of lectures, delivered year after year to successive generations of his pupils, upon its authenticity and inspiration. They were altogether remote from the subject; and afterwards, when I came to know what the difficulties of belief really were, I found that these essays, which were supposed to be a triumphant confutation of the sceptic, were a mere sword of lath. They never touched the question, and if any doubts suggested themselves to the audience, nobody dared to give them tongue, lest the expression of them should beget a suspicion of heresy. I remember also some lectures on the proof of the existence of God and on the argument from design; all of which, when my mind was once awakened, were as irrelevant as the chattering of sparrows. When I did not even know who or what this God was, and could not bring my lips to use the word with any mental honesty, of what service was the 'watch argument' to me? Very lightly did the President pass over all these initial difficulties of his religion. I see him now, a gentleman with lightish hair, with a most mellifluous voice and a most pastoral manner, reading his prim little tracts to us directed against the 'shallow infidel' who seemed to deny conclusions so obvious that we were certain he could not be sincere, and those of us who had never seen an infidel might well be pardoned for supposing that he must always be wickedly blind. About a dozen of these tracts settled the infidel and the whole mass of unbelief from the time of Celsus downwards. The President's task was all the easier because he knew nothing of German literature;* and, indeed, the word 'German' was a term of reproach signifying something very awful, although nobody knew exactly what it was. Systematic theology was the next science to which the President directed us. We used a sort of Calvinistic manual which began by setting forth that mankind was absolutely in God's power. He was our maker, and we had no legal claim whatever to any consideration from Him. The author then mechanically built up the Calvinistic creed, step by step, like a house of cards. Systematic theology was the great business of our academical life. We had to read sermons to the President in class, and no sermon was considered complete and proper unless it unfolded what was called the scheme of redemption from beginning to end. So it came to pass that about the Bible, as I have already said, we were in darkness. It was a magazine of texts, and those portions of it which contributed nothing in the shape of texts, or formed no part of the scheme, were neglected. Worse still, not a word was ever spoken to us telling us in what manner to strengthen the reason, to subdue the senses, or in what way to deal with all the varied diseases of that soul of man which we were to set ourselves to save. All its failings, infinitely more complicated than those of the body, were grouped as 'sin,' and for these there was one quack remedy. If the patient did not like the remedy, or got no good from it, the fault was his. It is remarkable that the scheme was never of the slightest service to me in repressing one solitary evil inclination; at no point did it come into contact with me. At the time it seemed right and proper that I should learn it, and I had no doubt of its efficacy; but when the stress of temptation was upon me, it never occurred to me, nor when I became a minister did I find it sufficiently powerful to mend the most trifling fault. In after years, but not till I had strayed far away from the President and his creed, the Bible was really opened to me, and became to me, what it now is, the most precious of books.

There were several small chapels scattered in the villages near the college, and these chapels were 'supplied,' as the phrase is, by the students. Those who were near the end of their course were also employed as substitutes for regular ministers when they were temporarily absent. Sometimes a senior was even sent up to London to take the place, on a sudden emergency, of a great London minister, and when he came back he was an object almost of adoration. The congregation, on the other hand, consisting in some part of country people spending a Sunday in town and anxious to hear a celebrated preacher, were not at all disposed to adore, when, instead of the great man, they saw 'only a student.' By the time I was nineteen I took my turn in 'supplying' the villages, and set forth with the utmost confidence what appeared to me to be the indubitable gospel. No shadow of a suspicion of its truth ever crossed my mind, and yet I had not spent an hour in comprehending, much less in answering, one objection to it. The objections, in fact, had never met me; they were over my horizon altogether. It is wonderful to think how I could take so much for granted; and not merely take it to myself and for myself, but proclaim it as a message to other people. It would be a mistake, however, to suppose that theological youths are the only class who are guilty of such presumption. Our gregarious instinct is so strong that it is the most difficult thing for us to be satisfied with suspended judgment. Men must join a party, and have a cry, and they generally take up their party and their cry from the most indifferent motives. For my own part I cannot be enthusiastic

about politics, except on rare occasions when
the issue is a very narrow one. There is so much
that requires profound examination, and it dis-
gusts me to get upon a platform and dispute with
ardent Radicals or Conservatives who know nothing about even the rudiments of history, political
economy, or political philosophy, without which
it is as absurd to have an opinion upon what are
called politics as it would be to have an opinion
upon an astronomical problem without having
learned Euclid. The more incapable we are of
thorough investigation, the wider and deeper are
the subjects upon which we busy ourselves, and
still more strange, the more bigoted do we become
in our conclusions about them; and yet it is not
strange, for he who by painful processes has found
yes and no alternate for so long that he is not sure
which is final, is the last man in the world, if he
for the present is resting in yes, to crucify another
who can get no further than no. The bigot is he
to whom no such painful processes have ever been
permitted.

The society amongst the students was very poor.
Not a single friendship formed then has remained
with me. They were mostly young men of no
education, who had been taken from the counter,
and their spiritual life was not very deep. In many
of them it did not even exist, and their whole
attention was absorbed upon their chances of
getting wealthy congregations or of making desir-

able matches. It was a time in which the world outside was seething with the ferment which had been cast into it by Germany and by those in England whom Germany had influenced, but not a fragment of it had dropped within our walls. I cannot call to mind a single conversation upon any but the most trivial topics, nor did our talk ever turn even upon our religion, so far as it was a thing affecting the soul, but only upon it as something subsidiary to chapels, 'causes,' deacons, and the like. The emptiness of some of my colleagues, and their worldliness, too, were almost incredible. There was one who was particularly silly. He was a blonde youth with greyish eyes, a mouth not quite shut, and an eternal simper upon his face. He never had an idea in his head, and never read anything except the denominational newspapers and a few well-known aids to sermonising. He was a great man at all tea-meetings, anniversaries, and parties. He was facile in public speaking, and he dwelt much upon the joys of heaven and upon such topics as the possibility of our recognising one another there. I have known him describe for twenty minutes, in a kind of watery rhetoric, the passage of the soul to bliss through death, and its meeting in the next world with those who had gone before. With all his weakness he was close and mean in money matters, and when he left college, the first thing he did was to marry a widow with a fortune. Before long he became one

of the most popular of ministers in a town much
visited by sick persons, with whom he was an
especial favourite. I disliked him—and specially
disliked his unpleasant behaviour to women. If I
had been a woman I should have spurned him for
his perpetual insult of inane compliments. He was
always dawdling after 'the sex,' which was one of
his sweet phrases, and yet he was not passionate.
Passion does not dawdle and compliment, nor is
it nasty, as this fellow was. Passion may burn like
a devouring flame; and in a few moments, like
flame, may bring down a temple to dust and ashes,
but it is earnest as flame, and essentially pure.

During the first two years at college my life
was entirely external. My heart was altogether
untouched by anything I heard, read, or did, although I myself supposed that I took an interest
in them. But one day in my third year, a day I
remember as well as Paul must have remembered
afterwards the day on which he went to Damascus,*
I happened to find amongst a parcel of books a
volume of poems in paper boards. It was called
'Lyrical Ballads,'*and I read first one and then the
whole book. It conveyed to me no new doctrine,
and yet the change it wrought in me could only
be compared with that which is said to have been
wrought on Paul himself by the Divine apparition.
Looking over the 'Lyrical Ballads' again, as I have
looked over it a dozen times since then, I can hardly
see what it was which stirred me so powerfully,

nor do I believe that it communicated much to me which could be put in words. But it excited a movement and a growth which went on till, by degrees, all the systems which enveloped me like a body gradually decayed from me and fell away into nothing. Of more importance, too, than the decay of systems was the birth of a habit of inner reference and a dislike to occupy myself with anything which did not in some way or other touch the soul, or was not the illustration or embodiment of some spiritual law. There is, of course, a definite explanation to be given of one effect produced by the 'Lyrical Ballads.' God is nowhere formally deposed, and Wordsworth would have been the last man to say that he had lost his faith in the God of his fathers. But his real God is not the God of the Church, but the God of the hills, the abstraction Nature, and to this my reverence was transferred. Instead of an object of worship which was altogether artificial, remote, never coming into genuine contact with me, I had now one which I thought to be real, one in which literally I could live and move and have my being, an actual fact present before my eyes. God was brought from that heaven of the books, and dwelt on the downs in the far-away distances, and in every cloud-shadow which wandered across the valley. Wordsworth unconsciously did for me what every religious reformer has done,—he re-created my Supreme Divinity; substituting a new and living spirit for

the old deity, once alive, but gradually hardened
into an idol.

What days were those of the next few years
before increasing age had presented preciser problems and demanded preciser answers; before all
joy was darkened by the shadow of on-coming
death, and when life seemed infinite! Those were
the days when through the whole long summer's
morning I wanted no companion but myself, provided only I was in the country, and when books
were read with tears in the eyes. Those were the
days when mere life, apart from anything which
it brings, was exquisite. In my own college I found
no sympathy, but we were in the habit of meeting
occasionally the students from other colleges, and
amongst them I met with one or two, especially
one who had undergone experiences similar to my
own. The friendships formed with these young
men have lasted till now, and have been the most
permanent of all the relationships of my existence.
I wish not to judge others, but the persons who to
me have proved themselves most attractive, have
been those who have passed through such a process as that through which I myself passed; those
who have had in some form or other an enthusiastic stage in their history, when the story of Genesis
and of the Gospels has been rewritten, when God
has visibly walked in the garden, and the Son of
God has drawn men away from their daily occu-
pations into the divinest of dreams. I have known

men—most interesting men—with far greater powers than any which I have possessed, men who have never been trammelled by a false creed, who have devoted themselves to science and acquired a great reputation, who have somehow never laid hold upon me like the man I have just mentioned. He failed altogether as a minister, and went back to his shop, but the old glow of his youth burns, and will burn for ever. When I am with him our conversation naturally turns on matters which are of profoundest importance: with others it may be instructive, but I leave them unmoved, and I trace the difference distinctly to that visitation, for it was nothing else, which came to him in his youth.

The effect which was produced upon my preaching and daily conversation by this change was immediate. It became gradually impossible for me to talk about subjects which had not some genuine connection with me, or to desire to hear others talk about them. The artificial, the merely miraculous, the event which had no inner meaning, no matter how large externally it might be, I did not care for. A little Greek mythological story was of more importance to me than a war which filled the newspapers. What, then, could I do with my theological treatises? It would be a mistake, however, to suppose that I immediately became formally heretical. Nearly every doctrine in the college creed had once had a natural origin in the necessities of human nature, and might therefore be so interpreted as to become a necessity again. To reach through to that original necessity; to explain the atonement as I believed it appeared to Paul, and the sinfulness of man as it appeared to the prophets, was my object. But it was precisely this reaching after a meaning which constituted heresy. The distinctive essence of our orthodoxy was not this or that dogma, but the acceptance of dogmas as communications from without, and not as born from within. Heresy began, and in fact was altogether present, when I said to myself that a mere statement of the atonement as taught in class was impossible for me, and that I must go back to Paul and his century, place myself in his position, and connect the atonement through him with something which I felt. I thus continued to use all the terms which I had hitherto used; but an uneasy feeling began to develop itself about me in the minds of the professors, because I did not rest in the 'simplicity' of the gospel. To me this meant its unintelligibility. I remember, for example, discoursing about the death of Christ. There was not a single word which was ordinarily used in the pulpit which I did not use,—satisfaction for sin, penalty, redeeming blood, they were all there,— but I began by saying that in this world there was no redemption for man but by blood; furthermore, the innocent had everywhere and in all time to suffer for the guilty. It had been objected that it was contrary to our notion of an all-loving Being that He should demand such a sacrifice; but, contrary or not, in this world it was true, quite apart from Jesus, that virtue was martyred every day, unknown and unconsoled, in order that the wicked might somehow be saved. This was part of the scheme of the world, and we might dislike it or not, we could not get rid of it. The consequences of my sin, moreover, are rendered less terrible by virtues not my own. I am literally saved from penalties because another pays the penalty for me. The atonement, and what it accomplished for man, were therefore a sublime summing up as it were of what sublime men have to do for their race; an exemplification, rather than a contradiction, of Nature herself, as we know her in our own experience. Now, all this was really intended as a defence of the atonement; but the President heard me that Sunday, and on the Monday he called me into his room. He said that my sermon was marked by considerable ability, but he should have been better satisfied if I had confined myself to setting forth as plainly as I could the 'way of salvation' as revealed in Christ Jesus. What I had urged might perhaps have possessed some interest for cultivated people; in fact, he had himself urged pretty much the same thing many years ago, when he was a young man, in a sermon he had preached at the Union meeting;* but I must recollect that in all probability my sphere of usefulness would lie amongst humble hearers, perhaps in an agricultural village or a small town, and that he did not think people of this sort would understand me if I talked over their heads as I had done the day before. What they wanted on a Sunday, after all the cares of the week, was not anything to perplex and disturb them; not anything which demanded any exercise of thought; but a repetition of the 'old story of which, Mr. Rutherford, you know, we never ought to get weary; an exhibition of our exceeding sinfulness; of our safety in the Rock of Ages, and there only; of the joys of the saints and the sufferings of those who do not believe.' His words fell on me like the hand of a corpse, and I went away much depressed. My sermon had excited me, and the man who of all men ought to have welcomed me, had not a word of warmth or encouragement for me, nothing but the coldest indifference, and even repulse.

It occurs to me here to offer an explanation of a failing of which I have been accused in later years, and that is secrecy and reserve. The real truth is, that nobody more than myself could desire self-revelation; but owing to peculiar tendencies in me, and peculiarity of education, I was always prone to say things in conversation which I found produced blank silence in the majority of those who listened to me, and immediate opportunity was taken by my hearers to turn to something trivial. Hence it came to pass that only when tempted by unmistakable sympathy could I be induced to express my real self on any topic of importance. It is a curious instance of the difficulty of diagnosing (to use a doctor's word) any spiritual disease, if disease this shyness may be called. People would ordinarily set it down to self-reliance, with no healthy need of intercourse. It was nothing of the kind. It was an excess of communicativeness, an eagerness to show what was most at my heart, and to ascertain what was at the heart of those to whom I talked, which made me incapable of mere fencing and trifling, and so often caused me to retreat into myself when I found absolute absence of response.

I am also reminded here of a dream which I had in these years of a perfect friendship. I always felt that, talk with whom I would, I left something unsaid which was precisely what I most wished to say. I wanted a friend who would sacrifice himself to me utterly, and to whom I might offer a similar sacrifice. I found companions for whom I cared, and who professed to care for me; but I was thirsting for deeper draughts of love than any which they had to offer; and I said to myself that if I were to die, not one of them would remember me for more than a week. This was not selfishness, for I longed to prove my devotion as well as to receive that of another. How this ideal haunted me! It made me restless and anxious at the sight of every new face, wondering whether at last I had found that for which I searched as if for the kingdom of heaven. It is superfluous to say that a friend of the kind I wanted never appeared, and disappointment after disappointment at last produced in me a cynicism which repelled people from me, and brought upon me a good deal of suffering. I tried men by my standard, and if they did not come up to it I rejected them; thus I prodigally wasted a good deal of the affection which the world would have given me. Only when I got much older did I discern the duty of accepting life as God has made it, and thankfully receiving any scrap of love offered to me, however imperfect it might be. I don't know any mistake which I have made which has cost me more than this; but at the same time I must record that it was a mistake for which, considering everything, I cannot much blame myself. I hope it is amended now. Now when it is getting late I recognise a higher obligation, brought home to me by a closer study of the New Testament. Sympathy or no sympathy, a man's love should no more fail towards his fellows than that love which spent itself on disciples who altogether misunderstood it, like the rain which falls on just and unjust alike.*

CHAPTER III

WATER LANE

I HAD now reached the end of my fourth year at college, and it was time for me to leave. I was sent down into the eastern counties to a congregation which had lost its minister, and was there 'on probation' for a month. I was naturally a good speaker, and as the 'cause' had got very low, the attendance at the chapel increased during the month I was there. The deacons thought they had a prospect of returning prosperity, and in the end I received a nearly unanimous invitation, which, after some hesitation, I accepted. One of the deacons, a Mr. Snale, was against me; he thought I was not 'quite sound;' but he was overruled. We shall hear more of him presently. After a short holiday I entered on my new duties. The town was one of those which are not uncommon in that part of the world. It had a population of about seven or eight thousand, and was a sort of condensation of the agricultural country round. There was one main street, consisting principally of very decent, respectable shops. Generally speaking, there were two shops of each trade; one which was patronised by the Church and Tories, and another by the Dissenters and Whigs. The inhabitants were divided into two distinct camps—of the Church and Tory camp the other camp knew nothing. On the other hand, the knowledge which each member of the Dissenting camp had of every other member was most intimate. The Dissenters were further split up into two or three different sects, but the main sect was that of the Independents. They, in fact, dominated every other. There was a small Baptist community, and the Wesleyans had a new red brick chapel in the outskirts; but for some reason or other the Independents were really the Dissenters, and until the 'cause' had dwindled, as before observed, all the Dissenters of any note were to be found on Sunday in their meeting-house in Water Lane. My predecessor had died in harness at the age of seventy-five. I never knew him, but from all I could hear he must have been a man of some power. As he got older, however, he became feeble; and after a course of three sermons on a Sunday for fifty years, what he had to say was so entirely anticipated by his congregation, that although they all maintained that the gospel, or, in other words, the doctrine of the fall, the atonement, and so forth, should continually be presented, and their minister also believed and acted implicitly upon the same theory, they fell away,—some to the Baptists, some to the neighbouring Independents about two miles off, and some to the Church, while a few 'went nowhere.' When I came I found that the deacons still remained true. They were the skeleton; but the flesh was so woefully emaciated, that on my first Sunday there were not above fifty persons in a building which would hold seven hundred. These deacons were four in number. One was an old farmer who lived in a village three miles distant. Ever since he was a boy he had driven over to Water Lane on Sunday. He and his family brought their dinner with them, and ate it in the vestry; but they never stopped till the evening, because of the difficulty of getting home on dark nights, and because they all went to bed in wintertime at eight o'clock. Morning and afternoon Mr. Catfield—for that was his name—gave out the hymns. He was a plain, honest man, very kind, very ignorant, never reading any book except the Bible, and barely a newspaper save *Bell's Weekly Messenger*.* Even about the Bible he knew little or nothing beyond a few favourite chapters; and I am bound to say that, so far as my experience goes, the character so frequently drawn in romances of intense Bible students in Dissenting congregations is very rare. At the same time Mr. Catfield believed himself to be very orthodox, and in his way was very pious. I could never call him a hypocrite. He was as sincere as he could be, and yet no religious expression of his was ever so sincere as the most ordinary expression of the most trifling pleasure or pain. The second deacon, Mr. Weeley, was, as he described himself, a builder and undertaker; more properly an undertaker and carpenter. He was a thin, tall man, with a tenor voice, and he set the tunes. He was entirely without energy of any kind, and always seemed oppressed by a world which was too much for him. He had depended a good deal for custom upon his chapel connection; and when the attendance at the chapel fell off, his trade fell off likewise, so that he had to compound with his creditors. He was a mere shadow, a man of whom nothing could be said either good or evil. The third deacon was Mr. Snale, the draper. When I first knew him he was about thirty-five. He was slim, small, and small-faced, closely shaven excepting a pair of little curly whiskers, and he was extremely neat. He had a little voice too, rather squeaky, and the marked peculiarity that he hardly ever said anything, no matter how disagreeable it might be, without stretching as if in a smile his thin little lips. He kept the principal draper's shop in the town, and even Church people spent their money with him, because he was so very genteel compared with the other draper, who was a great red man, and hung things outside his window. Mr. Snale was married, had children, and was strictly proper. But his way of talking to women and about them was more odious than the way of a debauchee. He invariably called them 'the ladies,' or more exactly, 'the leedies;' and he hardly ever spoke to a 'leedy' without a smirk and some faint attempt at a joke. One of the customs of the chapel was what were called Dorcas meetings. Once a month the wives and daughters drank tea with each other; the evening being ostensibly devoted to making clothes for the poor. The husband of the lady who gave the entertainment for the month had to wait upon the company, and the minister was expected to read to them while they worked. It was my lot to be Mr. Snale's guest two or three times when Mrs. Snale was the Dorcas hostess. We met in the drawing-room, which was over the shop, and looked out into the town market-place. There was a round table in the middle of the room, at which Mrs. Snale sat and made the tea. Abundance of hot buttered toast and muffins were provided, which Mr. Snale and a maid handed round to the party. Four pictures decorated the walls. One hung over the mantelpiece. It was a portrait in oils of Mr. Snale, and opposite to it, on the other side, was a portrait of Mrs. Snale. Both were daubs, but curiously faithful in depicting what was most offensive in the character of both the originals, Mr. Snale's simper being preserved; together with the peculiarly hard, heavy sensuality of the eye in Mrs. Snale, who was large and full-faced, correct like Mr. Snale, a member of the church, a woman whom I never saw moved to any generosity, and cruel, not with the ferocity of the tiger, but with the dull insensibility of a cart-wheel, which will roll over a man's neck as easily as over a flint. The third picture represented the descent of the Holy Ghost: a number of persons sitting in a chamber, and each one with the flame of a candle on his head. The fourth represented the last day. The Son of God was in a chair surrounded by clouds, and beside Him was a flying figure blowing a long mail-coach horn. The dead were coming up out of their graves; some were half out of the earth, others three-parts out—the whole of the bottom part of the picture being filled with bodies emerging from the ground, a few looking happy, but most of them very wretched; all of them being naked. The first time I went to Mrs. Snale's Dorcas gathering Mr. Snale was reader, on the ground that I was a novice; and I was very glad to resign the task to him. As the business in hand was week-day and secular, it was not considered necessary that the selected subjects should be religious: but as it was distinctly connected with the chapel, it was also considered that they should have a religious flavour. Consequently the Bible was excluded, and so were books on topics altogether worldly. Dorcas meetings were generally, therefore, shut up to the denominational journal and to magazines. Towards the end of the evening Mr. Snale read the births, deaths, and marriages in this journal. It would not have been thought right to read them from any other newspaper, but it was agreed, with a fineness of tact which was very remarkable, that it was quite right to read them in one which was 'serious.'* During the whole time that the reading was going on conversation was not arrested, but was conducted in a kind of half whisper; and this was another reason why I exceedingly disliked to read, for I could never endure to speak if people did not listen. At half-past eight the work was put away, and Mrs. Snale went to the piano and played a hymn tune, the minister having first of all selected the hymn. Singing over, he offered a short prayer, and the company separated. Supper was not served, as it was found to be too great an expense. The husbands of the ladies generally came to escort them home, but did not come upstairs. Some of the gentlemen waited below in the dining-room, but most of them preferred the shop, for, although it was shut, the gas was burning to enable the assistants to put away the goods which had been got out during the day. When it first became my turn to read I proposed the 'Vicar of Wakefield;'* but although no objection was raised at the time, Mr. Snale took an opportunity of telling me, after I had got through a chapter or two, that he thought it would be better if it were discontinued. 'Because, you know, Mr. Rutherford,' he said, with his smirk, 'the company is mixed; there are young leedies present, and *perhaps*, Mr. Rutherford, a book with a more requisite tone might be more suitable on such an occasion.' What he meant I did not know, and how to find a book with a more requisite tone I did not know. However, the next time, in my folly, I tried a selection from George Fox's Journal.*

Mr. Snale objected to this too. It was 'hardly of a character adapted for social intercourse,' he thought, and furthermore, 'although Mr. Fox might be a very good man, and was a converted character, yet he did not, you know, Mr. Rutherford, belong to us.' So I was reduced to that class of literature which of all others I most abominated, and which always seemed to me the most profane, —religious and sectarian gossip, religious novels designed to make religion attractive, and other slip-slop of this kind. I could not endure it, and was frequently unwell on Dorcas evenings.

The rest of the small congregation was of no particular note. As I have said before, it had greatly fallen away, and all who remained clung to the chapel rather by force of habit than from any other reason. The only exception was an old maiden lady and her sister, who lived in a little cottage about a mile out of the town. They were pious in the purest sense of the word, suffering much from ill-health, but perfectly resigned, and with a kind of tempered cheerfulness always apparent on their faces, like the cheerfulness of a white sky with a sun veiled by light and lofty clouds. They were the daughters of a carriage builder, who had left them a small annuity. Their house was one of the sweetest which I ever entered. The moment I found myself inside it, I became conscious of perfect repose. Everything was at rest; books, pictures, furniture, all breathed the same peace. Nothing in the house was new, but everything had been preserved with such care that nothing looked old. Yet the owners were not what is called old-maidish; that is to say, they were not superstitious worshippers of order and neatness. I remember Mrs. Snale's children coming in one afternoon when I was there. They were rough and ill-mannered, and left traces of dirty footmarks all over the carpet, which the two ladies noticed at once. But it made no difference to the treatment of the children, who had some cake and currant wine given to them, and were sent away rejoicing. Directly they had gone, the eldest of my friends asked me if I would excuse her; she would gather up the dirt before it was trodden about. So she brought a dust-pan and brush (the little servant was out) and patiently swept the floor. That was the way with them. Did any mischief befall them or those whom they knew; without blaming anybody, they immediately and noiselessly set about repairing it with that silent promptitude of nature which rebels not against a wound, but the very next instant begins her work of protection and recovery. The Misses Arbour (for that was their name) mixed but little in the society of the town. They explained to me that their health would not permit it. They read books —a few—but they were not books about which I knew very much, and they belonged altogether to an age preceding mine. Of the names which

had moved me, and of all the thoughts stirring in
the time, they had heard nothing. They greatly
admired Cowper,* a poet who then did not much
attract me.

The country near me was rather level, but
towards the west it rose into soft swelling hills,
between which were pleasant lanes. At about ten
miles distant eastward was the sea. A small river
ran across the High Street under a stone bridge;
for about two miles below us it was locked up for
the sake of the mills, but at the end of the two miles
it became tidal and flowed between deep and
muddy banks through marshes to the ocean. Almost all my walks were by the river-bank down
to these marshes, and as far on as possible till the
open water was visible. Not that I did not like
inland scenery: nobody could like it more, but the
sea was a corrective to the littleness all round me.
With the ships on it sailing to the other end of the
earth it seemed to connect me with the great world
outside the parochialism of the society in which
I lived.

Such was the town of C——, and such the company amidst which I found myself. After my probation it was arranged that I should begin my new
duties at once, and accordingly I took lodgings,
—two rooms over the shop of a tailor who acted
as chapel-keeper, pew-opener, and sexton. There
was a small endowment on the chapel of fifty
pounds a year, and the rest of my income was

derived from the pew-rents, which at the time I took charge did not exceed another seventy. The first Sunday on which I preached after being accepted was a dull day in November, but there was no dulness in me. The congregation had increased a good deal during the past four weeks, and I was stimulated by the prospect of the new life before me. It seemed to be a fit opportunity to say something generally about Christianity and its special peculiarities. I began by pointing out that each philosophy and religion which had arisen in the world was the answer to a question earnestly asked at the time; it was a remedy proposed to meet some extreme pressure. Religions and philosophies were not created by idle people who sat down and said, 'Let us build up a system of beliefs upon the universe; what shall we say about immortality, about sin?' and so on. Unless there had been antecedent necessity there could have been no religion; and no problem of life or death could be solved except under the weight of that necessity. The stoical morality arose out of the condition of Rome when the scholar and the pious man could do nothing but simply strengthen his knees and back to bear an inevitable burden. He was forced to find some counterpoise for the misery of poverty and persecution, and he found it in the denial of their power to touch him. So with Christianity. Jesus was a poor solitary thinker, confronted by two enormous and overpowering organisations, the Jewish hierarchy and the Roman state. He taught the doctrine of the kingdom of heaven; He trained Himself to have faith in the absolute monarchy of the soul, the absolute monarchy of His own; He tells us that each man should learn to find peace in his own thoughts, his own visions. It is a most difficult thing to do; most difficult to believe that my highest happiness consists in *my* perception of whatever is beautiful. If I by myself watch the sun rise, or the stars come out in the evening, or feel the love of man or woman, I ought to say to myself, 'There is nothing beyond this.' But people will not rest there; they are not content, and they are for ever chasing a shadow which flies before them, a something external which never brings what it promises. I said that Christianity was essentially the religion of the unknown and of the lonely; of those who are not a success. It was the religion of the man who goes through life thinking much, but who makes few friends and sees nothing come of his thoughts. I said a good deal more upon the same theme which I have forgotten. After the service was over I went down into the vestry. Nobody came near me but my landlord, the chapel-keeper, who said it was raining, and immediately went away to put out the lights and shut up the building. I had no umbrella, and there was nothing to be done but to walk out in the wet. When I got home I found that my supper, consisting of bread and cheese with a pint of beer, was on the table, but apparently it had been thought unnecessary to light the fire again at that time of night. I was overwrought, and paced about for hours in hysterics. All that I had been preaching seemed the merest vanity when I was brought face to face with the fact itself; and I reproached myself bitterly that my own creed would not stand the stress of an hour's actual trial. Towards morning I got into bed, but not to sleep; and when the dull daylight of Monday came, all support had vanished, and I seemed to be sinking into a bottomless abyss. I became gradually worse week by week, and my melancholy took a fixed form. I got a notion into my head that my brain was failing, and this was my first acquaintance with that most awful malady hypochondria. I did not know then what I know now, although I only half believe it practically, that this fixity of form is a frequent symptom of the disease, and that the general weakness manifests itself in a determinate horror, which gradually fades with returning health. For months—many months, this dreadful conviction of coming idiocy or insanity lay upon me like some poisonous reptile with its fangs driven into my very marrow, so that I could not shake it off. It went with me wherever I went, it got up with me in the morning, walked about with me all day, and lay down with me at night. I managed somehow or other to do my work, but I prayed incessantly for death; and to such a state was I reduced that I could not even make the commonest appointment for a day beforehand. The mere knowledge that something had to be done agitated me and prevented my doing it. In June next year my holiday came, and I went away home to my father's house. Father and mother were going for the first time in their lives to spend a few days by the seaside together, and I went with them to Ilfracombe. I had been there about a week, when on one memorable morning, on the top of one of those Devonshire hills, I became aware of a kind of flush in the brain and a momentary relief such as I had not known since that November night. I seemed, far away on the horizon, to see just a rim of olive light low down under the edge of the leaden cloud that hung over my head, a prophecy of the restoration of the sun, or at least a witness that somewhere it shone. It was not permanent, and perhaps the gloom was never more profound, nor the agony more intense, than it was for long after my Ilfracombe visit. But the light broadened and gradually the darkness was mitigated. I have never been thoroughly restored. Often, with no warning, I am plunged in the Valley of the Shadow,* and no outlet seems possible; but I contrive to traverse it, or to wait in calmness for access of strength. When I was at my worst I went to see a doctor. He recommended me stimulants. I had always been rather abstemious, and he thought I was suffering from physical weakness. At first wine gave me relief, and such marked relief that whenever I felt my misery insupportable I turned to the bottle. At no time in my life was I ever the worse for liquor, but I soon found the craving for it was getting the better of me. I resolved never to touch it except at night, and kept my vow; but the consequence was, that I looked forward to the night, and waited for it with such eagerness that the day seemed to exist only for the sake of the evening, when I might hope at least for rest. For the wine as wine I cared nothing; anything that would have dulled my senses would have done just as well. But now a new terror developed itself. I began to be afraid that I was becoming a slave to alcohol; that the passion for it would grow upon me, and that I should disgrace myself, and die the most contemptible of all deaths. To a certain extent my fears were just. The dose which was necessary to procure temporary forgetfulness of my trouble had to be increased, and might have increased dangerously. But one day, feeling more than usual the tyranny of my master, I received strength to make a sudden resolution to cast him off utterly. Whatever be the consequence, I said, I will not be the victim of this shame. If I am to go down to the grave, it shall be as a man, and I will bear what I have to bear honestly and without resort to the base evasion of stupefaction. So that night I went to bed having drunk nothing but water.

The struggle was not felt just then. It came later,
when the first enthusiasm of a new purpose had
faded away, and I had to fall back on mere force
of will. I don't think anybody but those who have
gone through such a crisis can comprehend what
it is. I never understood the maniacal craving
which is begotten by ardent spirits, but I understood enough to be convinced that the man who
has once rescued himself from the domination
even of half a bottle, or three-parts of a bottle of
claret daily, may assure himself that there is
nothing more in life to be done which he need
dread. Two or three remarks begotten of experience in this matter deserve record. One is, that
the most powerful inducement to abstinence, in
my case, was the interference of wine with liberty,
and above all things its interference with what I
really loved best, and the transference of desire
from what was most desirable to what was sensual
and base. The morning, instead of being spent
in quiet contemplation and quiet pleasures, was
spent in degrading anticipations. What enabled
me to conquer, was not so much heroism as a
susceptibility to nobler joys, and the difficulty
which a man must encounter who is not suscept-
ible to them must be enormous and almost insuper-
able. Pity, profound pity is his due, and especially
if he happen to possess a nervous, emotional
organisation. If we want to make men water-
drinkers, we must first of all awaken in them a

capacity for being tempted by delights which water-drinking intensifies. The mere preaching of self-denial will do little or no good. Another observation is, that there is no danger in stopping at once, and suddenly, the habit of drinking. The prisons and asylums furnish ample evidence upon that point, but there will be many an hour of exhaustion in which this danger will be simulated and wine will appear the proper remedy. No man, or at least very few men, would ever feel any desire for it soon after sleep. This shows the power of repose, and I would advise anybody who may be in earnest in this matter to be specially on guard during moments of physical fatigue, and to try the effect of eating and rest. Do not persist in a blind, obstinate wrestle. Simply take food, drink water, go to bed, and so conquer not by brute strength, but by strategy. Going back to hypochondria and its countless forms of agony, let it be borne in mind that the first thing to be aimed at is patience —not to get excited with fears, not to dread the evil which most probably will never arrive, but to sit down quietly and *wait*. The simpler and less stimulating the diet, the more likely it is that the sufferer will be able to watch through the wakeful hours without delirium, and the less likely is it that the general health will be impaired. Upon this point of health too much stress cannot be laid. It is difficult for the victim to believe that his digestion has anything to do with a disease which seems so purely spiritual, but frequently the misery will break up and yield, if it do not altogether disappear, by a little attention to physiology and by a change of air. As time wears on, too, mere duration will be a relief; for it familiarises with what at first was strange and insupportable, it shows the groundlessness of fears, and it enables us to say with each new paroxysm, that we have surmounted one like it before, and probably a worse.

CHAPTER IV

EDWARD GIBBON MARDON

I HAD now been 'settled,' to use a dissenting phrase, for nearly eighteen months. While I was ill I had no heart in my work, and the sermons I preached were very poor and excited no particular suspicion. But with gradually returning energy my love of reading revived, and questions which had slumbered again presented themselves. I continued for some time to deal with them as I had dealt with the atonement at college. I said that Jesus was the true Paschal Lamb,* for that by His death men were saved from their sins, and from the consequences of them; I said that belief in Christ, that is to say, a love for Him, was more powerful to redeem men than the works of the law. All this may have been true, but truth lies in relation. It was not true when I, understanding what I understood by it, taught it to men who professed to believe in the Westminster Confession.* The preacher who preaches it uses a vocabulary which has a certain definite meaning, and has had this meaning for centuries. He cannot stay to put his own interpretation upon it whenever it is upon his lips, and so his hearers are in a false position, and imagine him to be much more orthodox than he really is. For some time I fell into this snare, until one day I happened to be reading the story

of Balaam.* Balaam, though most desirous to pro-
phesy smooth things for Balak, had nevertheless
a word put into his mouth by God. When he
came to Balak he was unable to curse, and could
do nothing but bless. Balak, much dissatisfied,
thought that a change of position might alter
Balaam's temper, and he brought him away from
the high places of Baal to the field of Zophim, to
the top of Pisgah. But Balaam could do nothing
better even on Pisgah. Not even a compromise
was possible, and the second blessing was more
emphatic than the first. 'God,' cried the prophet,
pressed sorely by his message, 'is not a man, that
He should lie; neither the son of man, that He
should repent: hath He said, and shall He not do
it? or hath He spoken, and shall He not make it
good? Behold, I have received commandment to
bless: and He hath blessed; and I cannot reverse
it.' This was very unsatisfactory, and Balaam was
asked, if he could not curse, at least to refrain from
benediction. The answer was still the same. 'Told
not I thee, saying, All that the Lord speaketh, that
I must do'? A third shift was tried, and Balaam
went to the top of Peor. This was worse than
ever. The Spirit of the Lord came upon him, and
he broke out into triumphal anticipation of the
future glories of Israel. Balak remonstrated in
wrath, but Balaam was altogether inaccessible.
'If Balak would give me his house full of silver
and gold, I cannot go beyond the commandment

of the Lord, to do either good or bad of mine own mind; but what the Lord saith, that will I speak.' This story greatly impressed me, and I date from it a distinct disinclination to tamper with myself, or to deliver what I had to deliver in phrases which, though they might be conciliatory, were misleading.

About this time there was a movement in the town to obtain a better supply of water. The soil was gravelly and full of cesspools, side by side with which were sunk the wells. A public meeting was held, and I attended and spoke on behalf of the scheme. There was much opposition, mainly on the score that the rates would be increased, and on the Saturday after the meeting the following letter appeared in the *Sentinel*, the local paper:—

'SIR,—It is not my desire to enter into the controversy now raging about the water-supply of this town, but I must say I was much surprised that a minister of religion should interfere in politics. Sir, I cannot help thinking that if the said minister would devote himself to the Water of Life,—

> *"that gentle fount*
> *Progressing from Immanuel's mount,"*—

it would be much more harmonious with his function as a follower of him who knew nothing save Christ crucified. Sir, I have no wish to introduce controversial topics upon a subject like religion into your columns, which are allotted to a different line, but I must be permitted to observe that I fail to see how a minister's usefulness can be stimulated if he sets class against class. Like the widows in affliction of old, he should keep himself pure and unspotted*from the world. How can many of us accept the glorious gospel on the Sabbath from a man who will incur spots during the week by arguing about cesspools like any other man? Sir, I will say nothing, moreover, about a minister of the gospel assisting to bind burdens—that is to say, rates and taxation—upon the shoulders of men grievous to be borne. Surely, sir, a minister of the Lamb of God, who was shed for the remission of sins, should be *against* burdens.—I am, sir, your obedient servant,

A CHRISTIAN TRADESMAN.'

I had not the least doubt as to the authorship of this precious epistle. Mr. Snale's hand was apparent in every word. He was fond of making religious verses, and once we were compelled to hear the Sunday-school children sing a hymn which he had composed. The two lines of poetry were undoubtedly his. Furthermore, although he had been a chapel-goer all his life, he muddled, invariably, passages from the Bible. They had no definite meaning for him, and there was nothing, consequently, to prevent his tacking the end of one verse to the beginning of another. Mr. Snale, too, continually 'failed to see.' Where he got the phrase I do not know, but he liked it, and was always repeating it. However, I had no external evidence that it was he who was my enemy, and I held my peace. I was supported at the public meeting by a speaker from the body of the hall whom I had never seen before. He spoke remarkably well, was evidently educated, and I was rather curious about him.

It was my custom on Saturdays to go out for the whole of the day by the river, seawards, to prepare for the Sunday. I was coming home rather tired, when I met this same man against a stile. He bade me good-evening, and then proceeded to thank me for my speech, saying many complimentary things about it. I asked who it was to whom I had the honour of talking, and he told me he was Edward Gibbon Mardon.* 'It was Edward Gibson Mardon once, sir,' he said, smilingly. 'Gibson was the name of a rich old aunt who was expected to do something for me, but I disliked her, and never went near her. I did not see why I should be ticketed with her label, and as Edward Gibson was very much like Edward Gibbon, the immortal author of the "Decline and Fall," I dropped the "s" and stuck in a "b." I am nothing but a compositor on the *Sentinel*, and Saturday afternoon, after the paper is out, is a holiday for me, unless there is any reporting to do, for I have to turn my attention to that occa-

sionally.' Mr. Edward Gibbon Mardon, I observed, was slightly built, rather short, and had
scanty whiskers which developed into a little
thicker tuft on his chin. His eyes were pure blue,
like the blue of the speedwell. They were not
piercing, but perfectly transparent, indicative of
a character which, if it possessed no particular
creative power, would not permit self-deception.
They were not the eyes of a prophet, but of a
man who would not be satisfied with letting a
half-known thing alone and saying he believed it.
His lips were thin, but not compressed into bitterness; and above everything there was in his face
a perfectly legible frankness, contrasting pleasantly
with the doubtfulness of most of the faces I knew.
I expressed my gratitude to him for his kind
opinion, and as we loitered he said—

'Sorry to see that attack upon you in the *Sentinel*.
I suppose you are aware it was Snale's. Everybody could tell that who knows the man.'

'If it is Mr. Snale's, I am very sorry.'

'It is Snale's. He is a contemptible cur; and
yet it is not his fault. He has heard sermons about
all sorts of supernatural subjects for thirty years,
and he has never once been warned against meanness, so of course he supposes that supernatural
subjects are everything and meanness is nothing.
But I will not detain you any longer now, for you
are busy. Good-night, sir.'

This was rather abrupt and disappointing.

However, I was much absorbed in the morrow, and passed on.

Although I despised Snale, his letter was the beginning of a great trouble to me. I had now been preaching for many months, and had met with no response whatever. Occasionally a stranger or two visited the chapel, and with what eager eyes did I not watch for them on the next Sunday, but none of them came twice. It was amazing to me that I could pour out myself as I did, poor although I knew that self to be, and yet make so little impression. Not one man or woman seemed any different because of anything I had said or done, and not a soul kindled at any word of mine, no matter with what earnestness it might be charged. How I groaned over my incapacity to stir in my people any participation in my thoughts or care for them! Looking at the history of those days now from a distance of years, everything assumes its proper proportion. I was at work, it is true, amongst those who were exceptionally hard and worldly, but I was seeking amongst men (to put it in orthodox language) what I ought to have sought with God alone. In other, and perhaps plainer phrase, I was expecting from men a sympathy which proceeds from the Invisible only. Sometimes, indeed, it manifests itself in the long-postponed justice of time, but more frequently it is nothing more and nothing less than a consciousness of approval by the Unseen, a peace unspeakable, which is bestowed on us when self is suppressed. I did not know then how little one man can change another, and what immense and persistent efforts are necessary— efforts which seldom succeed except in childhood —to accomplish anything but the most superficial alteration of character. Stories are told of sudden conversions, and of course if a poor simple creature can be brought to believe that hell-fire awaits him as the certain penalty of his misdeeds, he will cease to do them; but this is no real conversion, for essentially he remains pretty much the same kind of being that he was before.

I remember while this mood was on me, that I was much struck with the absolute loneliness of Jesus, and with His horror of that death upon the cross. He was young and full of enthusiastic hope, but when He died He had found hardly anything but misunderstanding. He had written nothing, so that He could not expect that His life would live after Him. Nevertheless His confidence in His own errand had risen so high, that He had not hesitated to proclaim Himself the Messiah: not the Messiah the Jews were expecting, but still the Messiah. I dreamed over His walks by the lake, over the deeper solitude of His last visit to Jerusalem, and over the gloom of that awful Friday afternoon.* The hold which He has upon us is easily explained, apart from the dignity of His recorded sayings and the purity of His life.

There is no Saviour for us like the hero who has passed triumphantly through the distress which troubles *us*. Salvation is the spectacle of a victory by another over foes like our own. The story of Jesus is the story of the poor and forgotten. He is not the Saviour for the rich and prosperous, for they want no Saviour. The healthy, active, and well-to-do need Him not, and require nothing more than is given by their own health and prosperity. But every one who has walked in sadness because his destiny has not fitted his aspirations; every one who, having no opportunity to lift himself out of his little narrow town or village circle of acquaintances, has thirsted for something beyond what they could give him; everybody who, with nothing but a dull, daily round of mechanical routine before him, would welcome death, if it were martyrdom for a cause; every humblest creature, in the obscurity of great cities or remote hamlets, who silently does his or her duty without recognition—all these turn to Jesus, and find themselves in Him. He died, faithful to the end, with infinitely higher hopes, purposes, and capacity than mine, and with almost no promise of anything to come of them.

Something of this kind I preached one Sunday, more as a relief to myself than for any other reason. Mardon was there, and with him a girl whom I had not seen before. My sight is rather short, and I could not very well tell what she was like. After

the service was over he waited for me, and said
he had done so to ask me if I would pay him a
visit on Monday evening. I promised to do so,
and accordingly went. I found him living in a
small brick-built cottage near the outskirts of the
town, the rental of which I should suppose would
be about seven or eight pounds a year. There was
a patch of ground in front and a little garden
behind, a kind of narrow strip about fifty feet
long, separated from the other little strips by iron
hurdles. Mardon had tried to keep his garden in
order, and had succeeded, but his neighbour was
disorderly, and had allowed weeds to grow, black-
ing bottles and old tin cans to accumulate, so that
whatever pleasure Mardon's labours might have
afforded was somewhat spoiled. He himself came
to the door when I knocked, and I was shown
into a kind of sitting-room with a round table in
the middle and furnished with Windsor chairs,*
two arm-chairs of the same kind standing on
either side the fireplace. Against the window was
a smaller table with a green baize tablecloth, and
about half-a-dozen plants stood on the window-
sill serving as a screen. In the recess on one side
of the fireplace was a cupboard, upon the top of
which stood a tea-caddy, a workbox, some tum-
blers, and a decanter full of water; the other side
being filled with a bookcase and books. There
were two or three pictures on the walls; one was
a portrait of Voltaire, another of Lord Bacon, and

a third was Albert Dürer's St. Jerome. This latter was an heirloom, and greatly prized I could perceive, as it was hung in the place of honour over the mantelpiece. After some little introductory talk, the same girl whom I had noticed with Mardon at the chapel came in, and I was introduced to her as his only daughter Mary. She began to busy herself at once in getting the tea. She was under the average height for a woman, and delicately built. Her head was small, but the neck was long. Her hair was brown, of a peculiarly lustrous tint, partly due to nature, but also to a looseness of arrangement and a most diligent use of the brush, so that the light fell not upon a dead compact mass, but upon myriads of individual hairs, each of which reflected the light. Her eyes, so far as I could make out, were a kind of greenish grey, but the eyelashes were long, so that it was difficult exactly to discover what was underneath them. The hands were small, and the whole figure exquisitely graceful; the plain black dress, which she wore fastened right up to the throat, suiting her to perfection. Her face, as I first thought, did not seem indicative of strength. The lips were thin, but not straight, the upper lip showing a remarkable curve in it. Nor was it a handsome face. The complexion was not sufficiently transparent, nor were the features regular. During tea she spoke very little, but I noticed one peculiarity about her manner of talking, and that was its perfect simplicity. There was no sort of effort or strain in anything she said, no attempt by emphasis of words to make up for weakness of thought, and no compliance with that vulgar and most disagreeable habit of using intense language to describe what is not intense in itself. Her yea was yea, and her no, no. I observed also that she spoke without disguise, although she was not rude. The manners of the cultivated classes are sometimes very charming, and more particularly their courtesy, which puts the guest so much at his ease, and constrains him to believe that an almost personal interest is taken in his affairs, but after a time it becomes wearisome. It is felt to be nothing but courtesy, the result of a rule of conduct uniform for all, and verging very closely upon hypocrisy. We long rather for plainness of speech, for some intimation of the person with whom we are talking, and that the mask and gloves may be laid aside. Tea being over, Miss Mardon cleared away the tea-things, and presently came back again. She took one of the arm-chairs by the side of the fireplace, which her father had reserved for her, and while he and I were talking, she sat with her head leaning a little sideways on the back of the chair. I could just discern that her feet, which rested on the stool, were very diminutive, like her hands. The talk with Mardon turned upon the chapel. I had begun it by saying that I had noticed him there on the Sunday just mentioned.

He then explained why he never went to any place of worship. A purely orthodox preacher it was, of course, impossible for him to hear, but he doubted also the efficacy of preaching. What could be the use of it, supposing the preacher no longer to be a believer in the common creeds? If he turns himself into a mere lecturer on all sorts of topics, he does nothing more than books do, and they do it much better. He must base himself upon the Bible, and above all upon Christ, and how can he base himself upon a myth? We do not know that Christ ever lived, or that if He lived His life was anything like what is attributed to Him. A mere juxtaposition of the Gospels shows how the accounts of His words and deeds differ according to the tradition followed by each of His biographers. I interrupted Mardon at this point by saying that it did not matter whether Christ actually existed or not. What the four evangelists recorded was eternally true, and the Christ-idea was true whether it was ever incarnated or not in a being bearing His name. 'Pardon me,' said Mardon, 'but it does very much matter. It is all the matter whether we are dealing with a dream or with reality. I can dream about a man's dying on the cross in homage to what he believed, but I would not perhaps die there myself; and when I suffer from hesitation whether I ought to sacrifice myself for the truth, it is of immense assistance to me to know that a greater sacrifice has been made

before me—that a greater sacrifice is possible. To
know that somebody has poetically imagined
that it is possible, and has very likely been altogether incapable of its achievement, is no help.
Moreover, the commonplaces which even the most
freethinking of Unitarians seem to consider as
axiomatic, are to me far from certain, and even
unthinkable. For example, they are always talking about the omnipotence of God. But power
even of the supremest kind necessarily implies an
object—that is to say, resistance. Without an
object which resists it, it would be a blank, and
what then is the meaning of omnipotence? It is
not that it is merely inconceivable; it is nonsense,
and so are all these abstract, illimitable, self-
annihilative attributes of which God is made up.'

This negative criticism, in which Mardon greatly
excelled, was all new to me, and I had no reply
to make. He had a sledgehammer way of expres-
sing himself, while I, on the contrary, always required time to bring into shape what I saw. Just
then I saw nothing; I was stunned, bewildered,
out of the sphere of my own thoughts, and pained
at the roughness with which he treated what I had
cherished. I was presently relieved, however, of
further reflection by Mardon's asking his daughter
whether her face was better. It turned out that
all the afternoon and evening she had suffered
greatly from neuralgia. She had said nothing
about it while I was there, but had behaved with

cheerfulness and freedom. Mentally I had accused her of slightness, and inability to talk upon the subjects which interested Mardon and myself; but when I knew she had been in torture all the time, my opinion was altered. I thought how rash I had been in judging her as I continually judged other people, without being aware of everything they had to pass through; and I thought, too, that if I had a fit of neuralgia, everybody near me would know it, and be almost as much annoyed by me as I myself should be by the pain. It is curious, also, that when thus proclaiming my troubles I often considered my eloquence meritorious, or, at least, a kind of talent for which I ought to praise God, contemning rather my silent friends as something nearer than myself to the expressionless animals. To parade my toothache, describing it with unusual adjectives, making it felt by all the company in which I might happen to be, was to me an assertion of my superior nature. But, looking at Mary, and thinking about her as I walked home, I perceived that her ability to be quiet, to subdue herself, to resist the temptation for a whole evening of drawing attention to herself by telling us what she was enduring, was heroism, and that my contrary tendency was pitiful vanity. I perceived that such virtues as patience and self-denial—which, clad in russet dress, I had often passed by unnoticed when I had found them amongst the poor or the humble—were more precious and more ennobling to their possessor than poetic yearnings, or the power to propound rhetorically to the world my grievances or agonies.

Miss Mardon's face was getting worse, and as by this time it was late, I stayed but a little while longer.

CHAPTER V

MISS ARBOUR

FOR some months I continued without much change in my monotonous existence. I did not see Mardon often, for I rather dreaded him. I could not resist him, and I shrank from what I saw to be inevitably true when I talked to him. I can hardly say it was cowardice. Those may call it cowardice to whom all associations are nothing, and to whom beliefs are no more than matters of indifferent research; but as for me, Mardon's talk darkened my days and nights. I never could understand the light manner in which people will discuss the gravest questions, such as God, and the immortality of the soul. They gossip about them over their tea, write and read review articles about them, and seem to consider affirmation or negation of no more practical importance than the conformation* of a beetle. With me the struggle to retain as much as I could of my creed was tremendous. The dissolution of Jesus into mythologic vapour was nothing less than the death of a friend dearer to me then than any other friend whom I knew. But the worst stroke of all was that which fell upon the doctrine of a life beyond the grave. In theory I had long despised the notion that we should govern our conduct here by hope of reward or fear of punishment hereafter.

But under Mardon's remorseless criticism, when he insisted on asking for the where and how, and pointed out that all attempts to say where and how ended in nonsense, my hope began to fail, and I was surprised to find myself incapable of living with proper serenity if there was nothing but blank darkness before me at the end of a few years. As I got older I became aware of the folly of this perpetual reaching after the future, and of drawing from to-morrow, and from to-morrow only, a reason for the joyfulness of to-day. I learned, when, alas! it was almost too late, to live in each moment as it passed over my head, believing that the sun as it is now rising is as good as it will ever be, and blinding myself as much as possible to what may follow. But when I was young I was the victim of that illusion, implanted for some purpose or other in us by Nature, which causes us, on the brightest morning in June, to think immediately of a brighter morning which is to come in July. I say nothing, now, for or against the doctrine of immortality. All I say is, that men have been happy without it, even under the pressure of disaster, and that to make immortality a sole spring of action here is an exaggeration of the folly which deludes us all through life with endless expectation, and leaves us at death without the thorough enjoyment of a single hour.

So I shrank from Mardon, but none the less did the process of excavation go on. It often happens that a man loses faith without knowing it. Silently the foundation is sapped while the building stands fronting the sun, as solid to all appearance as when it was first turned out of the builder's hands, but at last it falls suddenly with a crash. It was so at this time with a personal relationship of mine, about which I have hitherto said nothing. Years ago, before I went to college, and when I was a teacher in the Sunday-school, I had fallen in love with one of my fellow-teachers, and we became engaged. She was the daughter of one of the deacons. She had a smiling, pretty, vivacious face; was always somehow foremost in school treats, picnics, and chapel-work, and she had a kind of piquant manner, which to many men is more ensnaring than beauty. She never read anything; she was too restless and fond of outward activity for that, and no questions about orthodoxy or heresy ever troubled her head. We continued our correspondence regularly after my appointment as minister, and her friends, I knew, were looking to me to fix a day for marriage. But although we had been writing to one another as affectionately as usual, a revolution had taken place. I was quite unconscious of it, for we had been betrothed for so long that I never once considered the possibility of any rupture. One Monday morning, however, I had a letter from her. It was not often that she wrote on Sunday, as she had a religious prejudice against writing letters on that day. However, this was urgent, for it was to tell me that an aunt of hers who was staying at her father's was just dead, and that her uncle wanted her to go and live with him for some time, to look after the little children who were left behind. She said that her dear aunt died a beautiful death, trusting in the merits of the Redeemer. She also added, in a very delicate way, that she would have agreed to go to her uncle's at once, but she had understood that we were to be married soon, and she did not like to leave home for long. She was evidently anxious for me to tell her what to do. This letter, as I have said, came to me on Monday, when I was exhausted by a more than usually desolate Sunday. I became at once aware that my affection for her, if it ever really existed, had departed. I saw before me the long days of wedded life with no sympathy, and I shuddered when I thought what I should do with such a wife. How could I take her to Mardon? How could I ask him to come to me? Strange to say, my pride suffered most. I could have endured, I believe, even discord at home, if only I could have had a woman whom I could present to my friends, and whom they would admire. I was never unselfish in the way in which women are, and yet I have always been more anxious that people should respect my wife than respect me, and at any time would withdraw myself into the shade if only she might be brought into the light. This is nothing noble. It is an obscure form of egotism probably, but anyhow, such always was my case. It took but a very few hours to excite me to distraction. I had gone on for years without realising what I saw now, and although in the situation itself the change had been only gradual, it instantaneously became intolerable. Yet I never was more incapable of acting. What could I do? After such a long betrothal, to break loose from her would be cruel and shameful. I could never hold up my head again, and in the narrow circle of Independency, the whole affair would be known and my prospects ruined. Then other and subtler reasons presented themselves. No men can expect ideal attachments. We must be satisfied with ordinary humanity. Doubtless my friend with a lofty imagination would be better matched with some Antigone who exists somewhere and whom he does not know. But he wisely does not spend his life in vain search after her, but settles down with the first decently sensible woman he finds in his own street, and makes the best of his bargain. Besides, there was the power of use and wont to be considered. Ellen had no vice of temper, no meanness, and it was not improbable that she would be just as good a help-meet for me in time as I had a right to ask. Living together, we should mould one another, and at last like one another. Marrying her, I should be relieved from the insufferable solitude which was depressing me to death, and should have a home. So it has always been with me. When there has been the sternest need of promptitude, I have seen such multitudes of arguments for and against every course that I have despaired. I have at my command any number of maxims, all of them good, but I am powerless to select the one which ought to be applied. A general principle, a fine saying, is nothing but a tool, and the wit of man is shown not in his possession of a well-furnished tool-chest, but in the ability to pick out the proper instrument and use it. I remained in this miserable condition for days, not venturing to answer Ellen's letter, until at last I turned out for a walk. I have often found that motion and change will bring light and resolution when thinking will not. I started off in the morning down by the river, and towards the sea, my favourite stroll. I went on and on under a leaden sky, through the level, solitary, marshy meadows, where the river began to lose itself in the ocean, and I wandered about there, struggling for guidance. In my distress I actually knelt down and prayed, but the heavens remained impassive as before, and I was half ashamed of what I had done, as if it were a piece of hypocrisy. At last, wearied out, I turned homeward, and diverging from the direct road, I was led past the house where the Misses Arbour lived. I was faint, and some beneficent inspiration prompted me to call. I went in, and found that the younger of the two sisters was out. A sudden tendency to hysterics overcame me, and I asked for a glass of water. Miss Arbour, having given it to me, sat down by the side of the fireplace opposite to the one at which I was sitting, and for a few moments there was silence. I made some commonplace observation, but instead of answering me she said quietly, 'Mr. Rutherford, you have been upset; I hope you have met with no accident.' How it came about I do not know, but my whole story rushed to my lips, and I told her all of it with quivering voice. I cannot imagine what possessed me to make her my confidante. Shy, reserved, and proud, I would have died rather than have breathed a syllable of my secret if I had been in my ordinary humour, but her soft, sweet face altogether overpowered me. As I proceeded with my tale, the change that came over her was most remarkable. When I began she was leaning back placidly in her large chair, with her handkerchief upon her lap; but gradually her face kindled, she sat upright, and she was transformed with a completeness and suddenness which I could not have conceived possible. At last, when I had finished, she put both her hands to her forehead, and almost shrieked out, 'Shall I tell him?—O my God, shall I tell him?—may God have mercy on him!' I was amazed beyond measure at the altogether unsuspected depth of passion which was revealed in her whom I had never before seen disturbed by more than a ripple of emotion. She drew her chair nearer to mine, put both her hands on my knees, looked right into my eyes, and said, 'Listen.' She then moved back a little, and spoke as follows:—

'It is forty-five years ago this month since I was married. You are surprised; you have always known me under my maiden name, and you thought I had always been single. It is forty-six years ago this month since the man who afterwards became my husband first saw me. He was a partner in a cloth firm. At that time it was the duty of one member of a firm to travel, and he came to our town, where my father was a well-to-do carriage-builder. My father was an old customer of his house, and the relationship between the customer and the wholesale merchant was then very different from what it is now. Consequently, Mr. Hexton—for that was my husband's name—was continually asked to stay with us so long as he remained in the town. He was what might be called a singularly handsome man, that is to say, he was upright, well-made, with a straight nose, black hair, dark eyes, and a good complexion. He dressed with perfect neatness and good taste, and had the reputation of being a most temperate and most moral man, much respected amongst the sect to which both of us belonged. When he first came our way I was about nineteen and he about three-and-twenty. My father and his had long been acquainted, and he was of

course received even with cordiality. I was excit-
able, a lover of poetry, a reader of all sorts of
books, and much given to enthusiasm. Ah! you
do not think so, you do not see how that can have
been, but you do not know how unaccountable
is the development of the soul, and what is the
meaning of any given form of character which
presents itself to you. You see nothing but the
peaceful, long since settled result, but how it came
there, what its history has been, you cannot tell.
It may always have been there, or have gradually
grown so, in gradual progress from seed to flower,
or it may be the final repose of tremendous forces.
I will show you what I was like at nineteen,' and
she got up and turned to a desk, from which she
took a little ivory miniature. 'That,' she said, 'was
given to Mr. Hexton when we were engaged. I
thought he would have locked it up, but he used
to leave it about, and one day I found it in the
dressing-table drawer, with some brushes and
combs, and two or three letters of mine. I with-
drew it, and burnt the letters. He never asked for
it, and here it is.' The head was small and set
upon the neck like a flower, but not bending
pensively. It was rather thrown back with a kind
of firmness, and with a peculiarly open air, as if
it had nothing to conceal and wished the world to
conceal nothing. The body was shown down to
the waist, and was slim and graceful. But what
was most noteworthy about the picture was its

solemn seriousness, a seriousness capable of infinite
affection, and of infinite abandonment, not sensuous abandonment—everything was too severe, too
much controlled by the arch of the top of the head
for that—but of an abandonment to spiritual aims.
Miss Arbour continued: 'Mr. Hexton after a while
gave me to understand that he was my admirer,
and before six months of acquaintanceship had
passed my mother told me that he had requested
formally that he might be considered as my suitor.
She put no pressure upon me, nor did my father,
excepting that they said that if I would accept
Mr. Hexton they would be content, as they knew
him to be a very well-conducted young man, a
member of the church, and prosperous in his
business. My first, and for a time my sovereign,
impulse was to reject him, because I thought him
mean, and because I felt he lacked sympathy with
me. Unhappily I did not trust that impulse. I
looked for something more authoritative, but I
was mistaken, for the voice of God, to me at least,
hardly ever comes in thunder, but I have to listen
with perfect stillness to make it out. It spoke to
me, told me what to do, but I argued with it and
was lost. I was guiltless of any base motive, but
I found the wrong name for what displeased me
in Mr. Hexton, and so I deluded myself. I
reasoned that his meanness was justifiable economy, and that his dissimilarity from me was
perhaps the very thing which ought to induce me

to marry him, because he would correct my failings. I knew I was too inconsiderate, too rash, too flighty, and I said to myself that his soberness would be a good thing for me. Oh, if I had but the power to write a book which should go to the ends of the world, and warn young men and women not to be led away by any sophistry when choosing their partners for life! It may be asked, How are we to distinguish heavenly instigation from hellish temptation? I say, that neither you nor I, sitting here, can tell how to do it. We can lay down no law by which infallibly to recognise the messenger from God. But what I do say is, that when the moment comes, it is perfectly easy for us to recognise him. Whether we listen to his message or not is another matter. If we do not—if we stop to dispute with him, we are undone, for we shall very soon learn to discredit him. So I was married, and I went to live in a dark manufacturing town, away from all my friends. I awoke to my misery by degrees, but still rapidly. I had my books sent down to me. I unpacked them in Mr. Hexton's presence, and I kindled at the thought of ranging my old favourites in my sitting-room. He saw my delight as I put them on some empty shelves, but the next day he said that he wanted a stuffed dog there, and that he thought my books, especially as they were shabby, had better go upstairs. We had to give some entertainments soon afterwards. The minister and his wife, with some other friends, came to tea, and the conversation turned on parties and the dulness of winter evenings if no amusements were provided. I maintained that rational human beings ought not to be dependent upon childish games, but ought to be able to occupy themselves and interest themselves with talk. Talk, I said,—not gossip, but talk, pleases me better than chess or forfeits; and the lines of Cowper*occurred to me—

> *"When one, that holds communion with the skies,*
> *Has filled his urn where these pure waters rise,*
> *And once more mingles with us meaner things,*
> *'Tis even as if an angel shook his wings;*
> *Immortal fragrance fills the circuit wide,*
> *That tells us whence his treasures are supplied."*

I ventured to repeat this verse, and when I had finished, there was a pause for a moment, which was broken by my husband's saying to the minister's wife, who sat next him, "O Mrs. Cook, I quite forgot to express my sympathy with you; I heard that you had lost your cat." The blow was deliberately administered, and I felt it as an insult. I was wrong, I know. I was ignorant of the ways of the world, and I ought to have been aware of the folly of placing myself above the level of my guests, and of the extreme unwisdom of revealing myself in that unguarded way to strangers. Two or three more experiences of that kind taught me to close myself carefully to all the world, and to beware how I uttered anything more than commonplace. But I was young, and ought to have been pardoned. I felt the sting of self-humiliation far into the night, as I lay and silently cried, while Mr. Hexton slept beside me. I soon found that he was entirely insensible to everything for which I most cared. Before our marriage he had affected a sort of interest in my pursuits, but in reality he was indifferent to them. He was cold, hard, and impenetrable. His habits were precise and methodical, beyond what is natural for a man of his years. I remember one evening—strange that these small events should so burn themselves into me—that some friends were at our house at tea. A tradesman in the town was mentioned, a member of our congregation, who had become bankrupt, and everybody began to abuse him. It was said that he had been extravagant; that he had chosen to send his children to the grammar-school, where the children of gentlefolk went; and finally, that only last year he had let his wife go to the seaside. I knew what the real state of affairs was. He had perhaps been living a little beyond his means, but as to the school, he had rather refined tastes, and he longed to teach his children something more than the ciphering, as it was called, and bookkeeping which they would have learned at the academy at which men in his position usually educated their boys: and as to the seaside his wife was ill, and he could

not bear to see her suffering in the smoky street,
when he knew that a little fresh air and change of
scene would restore her. So I said that I was sorry
to hear the poor man attacked; that he had done
wrong, no doubt, but so had the woman who was
brought before Jesus; and that with me, charity
or a large heart covered a multitude of sins. I
added that there was something dreadful in the
way in which everybody always seemed to agree
in deserting the unfortunate. I was a little moved,
and unluckily upset a teacup. No harm was done;
and if my husband, who sat next to me, had chosen
to take no notice, there need have been no disturb-
ance whatever. But he made a great fuss, crying,
"Oh, my dear, pray mind! Ring the bell instantly,
or it will all be through the tablecloth." In getting
up hastily to obey him, I happened to drag the
cloth, as it lay on my lap; a plate fell down and
was broken; everything was in confusion; I was
ashamed and degraded.

'I do not believe there was a single point in
Mr. Hexton's character in which he touched the
universal; not a single chink, however narrow,
through which his soul looked out of itself upon
the great world around. If he had kept bees, or
collected butterflies or beetles, I could have found
some avenue of approach. But he had no taste
for anything of the kind. He had his breakfast
at eight regularly every morning, and read his
letters at breakfast. He came home to dinner at

two, looked at the newspaper for a little while after dinner, and then went to sleep. At six he had his tea, and in half-an-hour went back to his counting-house, which he did not leave till eight. Supper at nine, and bed at ten, closed the day. It was a habit of mine to read a little after supper, and occasionally I read aloud to him passages which struck me, but I soon gave it up, for once or twice he said to me, "Now you've got to the bottom of that page, I think you had better go to bed," although perhaps the page did not end a sentence. But why weary you with all this? I pass over all the rest of the hateful details which made life insupportable to me. Suffice to say, that one wet Sunday evening, when we could not go to chapel and were in the dining-room alone, the climax was reached. My husband had a religious magazine before him, and I sat still doing nothing. At last, after an hour had passed without a word, I could bear it no longer, and I broke out—

'"James, I am wretched beyond description!"

'He slowly shut the magazine, tearing a piece of paper from a letter and putting it in as a mark, and then said—

'"What is the matter?"

'"You must know. You must know that ever since we have been married you have never cared for one single thing I have done or said; that is to say, you have never cared for me. It is *not* being married."

'It was an explosive outburst, sudden and almost incoherent, and I cried as if my heart would break.

'"What is the meaning of all this? You must be unwell. Will you not have a glass of wine?"

'I could not regain myself for some minutes, during which he sat perfectly still, without speaking, and without touching me. His coldness nerved me again, congealing all my emotion into a set resolve, and I said—

'"I want no wine. I am not unwell. I do not wish to have a scene. I will not, by useless words, embitter myself against you, or you against me. You know you do not love me. I know I do not love you. It is all a bitter, cursed mistake, and the sooner we say so and rectify it the better."

'The colour left his face; his lips quivered, and he looked as if he would have killed me.

'"What monstrous thing is this? What do you mean by your tomfooleries?"

'I did not speak.

'"Speak!" he roared. "What am I to understand by rectifying your mistake? By the living God, you shall not make me the laughing-stock and gossip of the town! I'll crush you first."

'I was astonished to see such rage develop itself so suddenly in him, and yet afterwards, when I came to reflect, I saw there was no reason for surprise. Self, self was his god, and the thought of the damage which would be done to him and his reputation was what roused him. I was still silent, and he went on—

'"I suppose you intend to leave me, and you think you'll disgrace me. You'll disgrace yourself. Everybody knows me here, and knows you've had every comfort and everything to make you happy. Everybody will say what everybody will have the right to say about you. Out with it and confess the truth, that one of your snivelling poets has fallen in love with you and you with him."

'I still held my peace, but I rose and went into the best bedchamber, and sat there in the dark till bedtime. I heard James come upstairs at ten o'clock as usual, go to his own room, and lock himself in. I never hesitated a moment. I could not go home to become the centre of all the chatter of the little provincial town in which I was born. My old nurse, who took care of me as a child, had got a place in London as housekeeper in a large shop in the Strand. She was always very fond of me, and to her instantly I determined to go. I came down, wrote a brief note to James, stating that after his base and lying sneer he could not expect to find me in the morning still with him, and telling him I had left him for ever. I put on my cloak, took some money which was my own out of my cashbox, and at half-past twelve heard the mail-coach approaching. I opened the front door softly—it shut with an oiled spring bolt; I went out, stopped the coach, and was presently

rolling over the road to the great city. Oh that
night! I was the sole passenger inside, and for
some hours I remained stunned, hardly knowing
what had become of me. Soon the morning began
to break, with such calm and such slow-changing
splendour that it drew me out of myself to look
at it, and it seemed to me a prophecy of the future.
No words can tell the bound of my heart at
emancipation. I did not know what was before
me, but I knew from what I had escaped; I did
not believe I should be pursued, and no sailor
returning from shipwreck and years of absence
ever entered the port where wife and children
were with more rapture than I felt journeying
through the rain into which the clouds of the
sunrise dissolved, as we rode over the dim flats of
Huntingdonshire southwards. There is no need
for me to weary you any longer, nor to tell you
what happened after I got to London, or how I
came here. I had a little property of my own,
and no child. To avoid questions I resumed my
maiden name. But one thing you must know,
because it will directly tend to enforce what I am
going to beseech of you. Years afterwards, I might
have married a man who was devoted to me. But
I told him I was married already, and not a word
of love must he speak to me. He went abroad in
despair, and I have never seen anything more
of him.

'You can guess now what I am going to pray

of you to do. Without hesitation, write to this girl and tell her the exact truth. Anything, any obloquy, anything friends or enemies may say of you must be faced even joyfully, rather than what I had to endure. Better die the death of the Saviour on the cross than live such a life as mine.'

I said: 'Miss Arbour, you are doubtless right, but think what it means. It means nothing less than infamy. It will be said, I broke the poor thing's heart, and marred her prospects for ever. What will become of me, as a minister, when all this is known?'

She caught my hand in hers, and cried with indescribable feeling—

'My good sir, you are parleying with the great Enemy of Souls.* Oh! if you did but know, if you *could* but know, you would be as decisive in your recoil from him, as you would from hell suddenly opened at your feet. Never mind the future. The one thing you have to do is the thing that lies next to you, divinely ordained for you. What does the 119th Psalm say?—"Thy word is a lamp unto my feet." We have no light promised us to show us our road a hundred miles away, but we have a light for the next footstep, and if we take that, we shall have a light for the one which is to follow. The inspiration of the Almighty could not make clearer to me the message I deliver to you. Forgive me—you are a minister, I know, and perhaps I ought not to speak so to you, but I am an old woman. Never would you have heard my history from me, if I had not thought it would help to save you from something worse than death.'

At this moment there came a knock at the door, and Miss Arbour's sister came in. After a few words of greeting I took my leave and walked home. I was confounded. Who could have dreamed that such tragic depths lay behind that serene face, and that her orderly precision was like the grass and flowers upon volcanic soil with Vesuvian* fires slumbering below? I had been altogether at fault, and I was taught, what I have since been taught over and over again, that unknown abysses, into which the sun never shines, lie covered with commonplace in men and women, and are revealed only by the rarest opportunity.

But my thoughts turned almost immediately to myself, and I could bring myself to no resolve. I was weak and tired, and the more I thought the less capable was I of coming to any decision. In the morning, after a restless night, I was in still greater straits, and being perfectly unable to do anything, I fled to my usual refuge, the sea. The whole day I swayed to and fro, without the smallest power to arbitrate between the contradictory impulses which drew me in opposite directions. I knew what I ought to do, but Ellen's image was ever before me, mutely appealing against her wrongs, and I pictured her deserted and with her life spoiled. I said to myself that instinct is all very well, but for what purpose is reason given to us if not to reason with it; and reasoning in the main is a correction of what is called instinct, and of hasty first impressions. I knew many cases in which men and women loved one another without similarity of opinions, and, after all, similarity of opinions upon theological criticism is a poor bond of union. But then, no sooner was this pleaded than the other side of the question was propounded with all its distinctness, as Miss Arbour had presented it. I came home thoroughly beaten with fatigue, and went to bed. Fortunately I sank at once to rest, and with the morning was born the clear discernment that whatever I ought to do, it was more manly of me to go than to write to Ellen. Accordingly, I made arrangements for getting somebody to supply my place in the pulpit for a couple of Sundays, and went home.

CHAPTER VI

ELLEN AND MARY

I NOW found myself in the strangest position. What was I to do? Was I to go to Ellen at once and say plainly, 'I have ceased to care for you'? I did what all weak people do. I wished that destiny would take the matter out of my hands. I would have given the world if I could have heard that Ellen was fonder of somebody else than me, although the moment the thought came to me I saw its baseness. But destiny was determined to try me to the uttermost, and make the task as difficult for me as it could be made. It was Thursday when I arrived, and somehow or other—how I do not know—I found myself on Thursday afternoon at her house. She was very pleased to see me, for many reasons. My last letters had been doubtful, and the time for our marriage, as she at least thought, was at hand. I, on my part, could not but return the usual embrace, but after the first few words were over there was a silence, and she noticed that I did not look well. Anxiously she asked me what was the matter. I said that something had been upon my mind for a long time, which I thought it my duty to tell her. I then went on to say that I felt she ought to know what had happened. When we were first engaged we both professed the same faith. From that faith

I had gradually departed, and it seemed to me that it would be wicked if she were not made acquainted before she took a step which was irrevocable. This was true, but it was not quite all the truth, and with a woman's keenness she saw at once everything that was in me. She broke out instantly with a sob—

'O Rough!' a nickname she had given me, 'I know what it all means—you want to get rid of me.'

God help me, if I ever endure greater anguish than I did then. I could not speak, much less could I weep, and I sat and watched her for some minutes in silence. My first impulse was to retract, to put my arms round her neck, and swear that whatever I might be, Deist or Atheist, nothing should separate me from her. Old associations, the thought of the cruel injustice put upon her, the display of an emotion which I had never seen in her before, almost overmastered me, and why I did not yield I do not know. Again and again have I failed to make out what it is which, in moments of extreme peril, has restrained me from making some deadly mistake, when I have not been aware of the conscious exercise of any authority of my own. At last I said—

'Ellen, what else was I to do? I cannot help my conversion to another creed. Supposing you had found out that you had married a Unitarian*and I had never told you!'

'O Rough! you are not a Unitarian, you don't love me,' and she sobbed afresh.

I could not plead against hysterics. I was afraid she would get ill. I thought nobody was in the house, and I rushed across the passage to get her some stimulants. When I came back her father was in the room. He was my aversion—a fussy, conceited man, who always prated about 'my daughter' to me in a tone which was very repulsive—just as if she were his property, and he were her natural protector against me.

'Mr. Rutherford,' he cried, 'what is the matter with my daughter? What have you said to her?'

'I don't think, sir, I am bound to tell you. It is a matter between Ellen and myself.'

'Mr. Rutherford, I demand an explanation. Ellen is mine. I am her father.'

'Excuse me, sir, if I desire not to have a scene here just now. Ellen is unwell. When she recovers she will tell you. I had better leave,' and I walked straight out of the house.

Next morning I had a letter from her father to say, that whether I was a Unitarian or not, my behaviour to Ellen showed I was bad enough to be one. Anyhow, he had forbidden her all further intercourse with me. When I had once more settled down in my solitude, and came to think over what had happened, I felt the self condemnation of a criminal without being able to accuse myself of a crime. I believe with Miss Arbour that it is madness for a young man who finds out he has made a blunder, not to set it right; no matter what the wrench may be. But that Ellen was a victim I do not deny. If any sin, however, was committed against her, it was committed long before our separation. It was nine-tenths mistake and one-tenth something more heinous; and the worst of it is, that while there is nothing which a man does which is of greater consequence than the choice of a woman with whom he is to live, there is nothing he does in which he is more liable to self-deception.

On my return I heard that Mardon was ill, and that probably he would die. During my absence a contested election for the county had taken place, and our town was one of the polling-places. The lower classes were violently Tory. During the excitement of the contest the mob had set upon Mardon as he was going to his work, and had reviled him as a Republican and an Atheist. By way of proving their theism they had cursed him with many oaths, and had so sorely beaten him that the shock was almost fatal. I went to see him instantly, and found him in much pain, believing that he would not get better, but perfectly peaceful. I knew that he had no faith in immortality, and I was curious beyond measure to see how he would encounter death without such a faith; for the problem of death, and of life after death, was still absorbing me even to the point of

monomania. I had been struggling as best I could
to protect myself against it, but with little success.
I had long since seen the absurdity and impossibility of the ordinary theories of hell and heaven.
I could not give up my hope in a continuance of
life beyond the grave, but the moment I came to
ask myself *how*, I was involved in contradictions.
Immortality is not really immortality of the person unless the memory abides and there be a connection of the self of the next world with the self
here, and it was incredible to me that there should
be any memories or any such connection after the
dissolution of the body; moreover, the soul, whatever it may be, is so intimately one with the body,
and is affected so seriously by the weaknesses,
passions, and prejudices of the body, that without
it my soul would not be myself, and the fable of
the resurrection of the body, of this same brain
and heart, was more than I could ever swallow in
my most orthodox days. But the greatest difficulty
was the inability to believe that the Almighty
intended to preserve all the mass of human beings,
all the countless millions of barbaric half-bestial
forms which, since the appearance of man, had
wandered upon the earth, savage or civilised. Is
it like Nature's way to be so careful about indivi-
duals, and is it to be supposed that, having produced, millions of years ago, a creature scarcely
nobler than the animals he tore with his fingers,
she should take pains to maintain him in existence

for evermore? The law of the universe everywhere is rather the perpetual rise from the lower to the higher; an immortality of aspiration after more perfect types; a suppression and happy forgetfulness of its comparative failures. There was nevertheless an obstacle to the acceptance of this negation in a faintness of heart which I could not overcome. Why this ceaseless struggle, if in a few short years I was to be asleep for ever? The position of mortal man seemed to me infinitely tragic. He is born into the world, beholds its grandeur and beauty, is filled with unquenchable longings, and knows that in a few inevitable revolutions of the earth he will cease. More painful still; he loves somebody, man or woman, with a surpassing devotion; he is so lost in his love that he cannot endure a moment without it; and when he sees it pass away in death, he is told that it is extinguished—that that heart and mind absolutely are *not*. It was always a weakness with me that certain thoughts preyed on me. I was always singularly feeble in laying hold of an idea, and in the ability to compel myself to dwell upon a thing for any lengthened period in continuous exhaustive reflection. But, nevertheless, ideas would frequently lay hold of *me* with such relentless tenacity that I was passive in their grasp. So it was about this time with death and immortality, and I watched eagerly Mardon's behaviour when the end had to be faced. As I have said, he was altogether calm. I did not like to question him while he was so unwell, because I knew that a discussion would arise which I could not control, and it might disturb him, but I would have given anything to understand what was passing in his mind.

During his sickness I was much impressed by Mary's manner of nursing him. She was always entirely wrapped up in her father, so much so, that I had often doubted if she could survive him; but she never revealed any trace of agitation. Under the pressure of the calamity which had befallen her, she showed rather increased steadiness, and even a cheerfulness which surprised me. Nothing went wrong in the house. Everything was perfectly ordered, perfectly quiet, and she rose to a height of which I had never suspected her capable, while her father's stronger nature was allowed to predominate. She was absolutely dependent on him. If he did not get well she would be penniless, and I could not help thinking that with the like chance before me, to say nothing of my love for him and anxiety lest he should die, I should be distracted, and lose my head; more especially if I had to sit by his bed, and spend sleepless nights such as fell to her lot. But she belonged to that class of natures which, although delicate and fragile, rejoice in difficulty. Her grief for her father was exquisite, but it was controlled by a sense of her responsibility. The greater the peril, the more complete was her self-command.

To the surprise of everybody Mardon got better. His temperate habits befriended him in a manner which amazed his more indulgent neighbours, who were accustomed to hot suppers, and whisky and water after them. Meanwhile I fell into greater difficulties than ever in my ministry. I wonder now that I was not stopped earlier. I was entirely unorthodox, through mere powerlessness to believe, and the catalogue of the articles of faith to which I might be said really to subscribe was very brief. I could no longer preach any of the dogmas which had always been preached in the chapel, and I strove to avoid a direct conflict by taking Scripture characters, amplifying them from the hints in the Bible, and neglecting what was supernatural. That I was allowed to go on for so long was mainly due to the isolation of the town and the ignorance of my hearers. Mardon and his daughter came frequently to hear me, and this, I believe, finally roused suspicion more than any doctrine expounded from the pulpit. One Saturday morning there appeared the following letter in the *Sentinel*:—

'Sir,—Last Sunday evening I happened to stray into a chapel not a hundred miles from Water Lane. Sir, it was a lovely evening, and

> "*The glorious stars on high,*
> *Set like jewels in the sky,*"*

were circling their courses, and, with the moon,

irresistibly reminded me of that blood which was shed for the remission of sins. Sir, with my mind attuned in that direction I entered the chapel. I hoped to hear something of that Rock of Ages*in which, as the poet sings, we shall wish to hide ourselves in years to come. But, sir, a young man, evidently a young man, occupied the pulpit, and great was my grief to find that the tainted flood of human philosophy had rolled through the town and was withering the truth as it is in Christ Jesus. Years ago that pulpit sent forth no uncertain sound, and the glorious gospel was proclaimed there—not a *German gospel*, sir—of our depravity and our salvation through Christ Jesus. Sir, I should like to know what the dear departed who endowed that chapel, and are asleep in the Lord in that burying-ground, would say if they were to rise from their graves and sit in those pews again and hear what I heard—a sermon which might have been a week-day lecture. Sir, as I was passing through the town, I could not feel that I had done my duty without announcing to you the fact as above stated, and had not raised a humble warning from—Sir, yours truly,

'A CHRISTIAN TRAVELLER.'

Notwithstanding the transparent artifice of the last paragraph, there was no doubt that the author of this precious production was Mr. Snale, and I at once determined to tax him with it. On the

Monday morning I called on him, and found him in his shop.

'Mr. Snale,' I said, 'I have a word or two to say to you.'

'Certainly, sir. What a lovely day it is! I hope you are very well, sir. Will you come upstairs?'

But I declined to go upstairs, as it was probable I might meet Mrs. Snale there. So I said that we had better go into the counting-house, a little place boxed off at the end of the shop, but with no door to it. As soon as we got in I began.

'Mr. Snale, I have been much troubled by a letter which has appeared in last week's *Sentinel*. Although disguised, it evidently refers to me, and to be perfectly candid with you, I cannot help thinking you wrote it.'

'Dear me, sir, may I ask *why* you think so?'

'The internal evidence, Mr. Snale, is overwhelming; but if you did not write it, perhaps you will be good enough to say so.'

Now Mr. Snale was a coward, but with a peculiarity which I have marked in animals of the rat tribe. He would double and evade as long as possible, but if he found there was no escape, he would turn and tear and fight to the last extremity.

'Mr. Rutherford, that is rather—ground of an, of an—what shall I say?—of an assumptive nature on which to make such an accusation, and I am not obliged to deny every charge which you may be pleased to make against me.'

'Pardon me, Mr. Snale, do you then consider what I have said is an accusation and a charge? Do you think that it was wrong to write such a letter?'

'Well, sir, I cannot exactly say that it was; but I must say, sir, that I do think it peculiar of you, peculiar of you, sir, to come here and attack one of your friends, who I am sure has always showed you so much kindness—to attack him, sir, with no proof.'

Now Mr. Snale had not openly denied his authorship. But the use of the word 'friend' was essentially a lie—just one of those lies which, by avoiding the form of a lie, have such a charm for a mind like his. I was roused to indignation.

'Mr. Snale, I will give you the proof which you want, and then you shall judge for yourself. The letter contains two lines of a hymn which you have misquoted. You made precisely that blunder in talking to the Sunday-school children on the Sunday before the letter appeared. You will remember that in accordance with my custom to visit the Sunday school occasionally, I was there on that Sunday afternoon.'

'Well, sir, I've not denied I did write it.'

'Denied you did write it!' I exclaimed, with gathering passion; 'what do you mean by the subterfuge about your passing through the town and by your calling me your friend a minute ago? What would you have thought if anybody had written anonymously to the *Sentinel*, and had accused you of selling short measure? You would have said it was a libel, and you would also have said that a charge of that kind ought to be made publicly and not anonymously. You seem to think, nevertheless, that it is no sin to ruin me anonymously.'

'Mr. Rutherford, I am sure I *am* your friend. I wish you well, sir, both here'—and Mr. Snale tried to be very solemn—'and in the world to come. With regard to the letter, I don't see it as you do, sir. But, sir, if you are going to talk in this tone, I would advise you to be careful. We have heard, sir,'—and here Mr. Snale began to simper and grin with an indescribably loathsome grimace,—'that some of your acquaintances in your native town are of opinion that you have not behaved quite so well as you should have done to a certain young lady of your acquaintance; and what is more, we have marked with pain here, sir, your familiarity with an atheist and his daughter, and we have noticed their coming to chapel, and we have also noticed a change in your doctrine since these parties attended there.'

At the word 'daughter' Mr. Snale grinned again, apparently to somebody behind me, and I found that one of his shopwomen had entered the counting-house, unobserved by me, while this conversation was going on, and that she was smirking in reply to Mr. Snale's signals. In a moment the

blood rushed to my brain. I was as little able to
control myself as if I had been shot suddenly
down a precipice.

'Mr. Snale, you are a contemptible scoundrel
and a liar.'

The effect on him was comical. He cried:
'What, sir!—what do you mean, sir?—a minister
of the gospel—if you were not, I would—a liar'—
and he swung round hastily on the stool on which
he was sitting, to get off and grasp a yard-measure
which stood against the fireplace. But the stool
slipped, and he came down ignominiously. I
waited till he got up, but as he rose a carriage
stopped at the door, and he recognised one of his
best customers. Brushing the dust off his trousers,
and smoothing his hair, he rushed out without
his hat, and in a moment was standing obsequi-
ously on the pavement bowing to his patron. I
passed him in going out, but the oily film of
subserviency on his face was not broken for an
instant.

When I got home I bitterly regretted what had
happened. I never regret anything more than the
loss of self-mastery. I had been betrayed, and yet
I could not for the life of me see how the betrayal
could have been prevented. It was upon me so
suddenly, that before a moment had been given
me for reflection, the words were out of my mouth.
I was distinctly conscious that the *I* had not said
those words. They had been spoken by some

other power working in me which was beyond my reach. Nor could I foresee how to prevent such a fall for the future. The only advice, even now, which I can give to those who comprehend the bitter pangs of such self-degradation as passion brings, is to watch the first risings of the storm, and to say 'Beware; be watchful,' at the least indication of a tempest. Yet, after every precaution, we are at the mercy of the elements, and in an instant the sudden doubling of a cape may expose us, under a serene sky, to a blast which, taking us with all sails spread, may overset us and wreck us irretrievably.

My connection with the chapel was now obviously at an end. I had no mind to be dragged before a church meeting, and I determined to resign. After a little delay I wrote a letter to the deacons, explaining that I had felt a growing divergence from the theology taught heretofore in Water Lane, and I wished consequently to give up my connection with them. I received an answer stating that my resignation had been accepted; I preached a farewell sermon; and I found myself one Monday morning with a quarter's salary in my pocket, a few bills to pay, and a blank outlook. What was to be done? My first thought was towards Unitarianism, but when I came to cast up the sum total of what I was assured, it seemed so ridiculously small that I was afraid. The occupation of a merely miscellaneous lecturer had always seemed to me very poor. I could not get up Sunday after Sunday and retail to people little scraps suggested by what I might have been studying during the week; and with regard to the great subjects, for the exposition of which the Christian minister specially exists—how much did I know about them? The position of a minister who has a gospel to proclaim; who can go out and tell men what they are to do to be saved, was intelligible; but not so the position of a man who had no such gospel. What reason for continuance as a preacher could I claim? Why should people hear me rather than read books? I was alarmed to find, on making my reckoning, that the older I got the less I appeared to believe. Nakeder and nakeder had I become with the passage of every year, and I trembled to anticipate the complete emptiness to which before long I should be reduced. What the dogma of immortality was to me I have already described, and with regard to God I was no better. God was obviously not a person in the clouds, and what more was really firm under my feet than this— that the universe is governed by immutable laws? These laws were not what is commonly understood as God. Nor could I discern any ultimate tendency in them. Everything was full of contradiction. On the one hand was infinite misery; on the other there were exquisite adaptations producing the highest pleasure: on the one hand the mystery of life-long disease, and on the other the equal mystery of the unspeakable glory of the sunrise on a summer's morning over a quiet summer sea. I happened to hear once an atheist discoursing on the follies of theism. If he had made the world, he would have made it much better. He would not have racked innocent souls with years of torture, that tyrants might live in splendour. He would not have permitted the earthquake to swallow up thousands of harmless mortals, and so forth. But, putting aside all dependence upon the theory of a coming rectification of such wrongs as these, the atheist's argument was shallow enough. It would have been easy to show that a world such as he imagines is unthinkable directly we are serious with our conception of it. On whatever lines the world may be framed, there must be *distinction*, *difference*, a higher and a lower; and the lower, relatively to the higher, must always be an evil. The *scale* upon which the higher and lower both are, makes no difference. The supremest bliss would not be bliss if it were not *definable* bliss, that is to say, in the sense that it has limits, marking it out from something else not so supreme. Perfectly uninterrupted, infinite light, without shadow, is a physical absurdity. I see a thing because it is lighted, but also because of the differences of light, or, in other words, because of shade, and without shade the universe would be objectless, and in fact invisible. The atheist was dreaming of shadowless light, a contradiction in terms. Mankind may be improved, and the improvement may be infinite, and yet good and evil must exist. So with death and life. Life without death is not life, and death without life is equally impossible. But though all this came to me, and was not only a great comfort to me, but prevented any shallow prating like that to which I listened from this lecturer, it could not be said that it was a gospel from which to derive apostolic authority. There remained morals. I could become an instructor of morality. I could warn tradesmen not to cheat, children to honour their parents, and people generally not to lie. The mission was noble, but I could not feel much enthusiasm for it, and more than this, it was a fact that reformations in morals have never been achieved by mere directions to be good, but have always been the result of an enthusiasm for some City of God, or some supereminent person. Besides, the people whom it was most necessary to reach would not be the people who would, unsolicited, visit a Unitarian meeting-house. As for a message of negations, emancipating a number of persons from the dogma of the Trinity or future punishment, and spending my strength in merely demonstrating the nonsense of orthodoxy, my soul sickened at the very thought of it. Wherein would men be helped, and wherein should I be helped? There were only two persons in the town who had ever been of any service to me. One was Miss

Arbour, and the other was Mardon. But I shrank from Miss Arbour, because I knew that my troubles had never been hers. She belonged to a past generation, and as to Mardon, I never saw him without being aware of the difficulty of accepting any advice from him. He was perfectly clear, perfectly secular, and was so definitely shaped and settled, that his line of conduct might always be predicted beforehand with certainty. I knew very well what he thought about preaching, and what he would tell me to do, or rather, what he would tell me not to do. Nevertheless, after all, I was a victim to that weakness which impels us to seek the assistance of others when we know that what they offer will be of no avail. Accordingly, I called on him. Both he and Mary were at home, and I was received with more than usual cordiality. He knew already that I had resigned, for the news was all over the town. I said I was in great perplexity.

'The perplexities of most persons arise,' said Mardon, 'as yours probably arise, from not understanding exactly what you want to do. For one person who stumbles and falls with a perfectly distinct object to be attained, I have known a score whose disasters are to be attributed to their not having made themselves certain what their aim is. You do not know what you believe, consequently you do not know how to act.'

'What would you do if you were in my case?'

'Leave the whole business and prefer the meanest

handicraft. You have no right to be preaching anything doubtful. You are aware what my creed is. I profess no belief in God, and no belief in what hangs upon it. Try and name now, any earnest conviction you possess, and see whether you have a single one which I have not got.'

'I *do* believe in God.'

'There is nothing in that statement. What do you believe about Him?—that is the point. You will find that you believe nothing, in truth, which I do not also believe of the laws which govern the universe and man.'

'I believe in an intellect of which these laws are the expression.'

'Now what kind of an intellect can that be? You can assign to it no character in accordance with its acts. It is an intellect, if it be an intellect at all, which will swallow up a city, and will create the music of Mozart for me when I am weary; an intellect which brings to birth His Majesty King George IV., and the love of an affectionate mother for her child; an intellect which, in the person of a tender girl, shows an exquisite conscience, and in the person of one or two religious creatures whom I have known, shows a conscience almost inverted. I have always striven to prove to my theological friends that their mere affirmation of God is of no consequence. They may be affirming anything or nothing. The question, the all-important question is, *What* can be affirmed about Him?'

'Your side of the argument naturally admits of a more precise statement than mine. I cannot encompass God with a well-marked definition, but for all that, I believe in Him. I know all that may be urged against the belief, but I cannot help thinking that the man who looks upon the stars, or the articulation of a leaf, is irresistibly impelled, unless he has been corrupted by philosophy, to say, There is intellect there. It is the instinct of the child and of the man.'

'I don't think so; but grant it, and again I ask, *What* intellect is it?'

'Again I say, I do not know.'

'Then why dispute? Why make such a fuss about it?'

'It really seems to me of immense importance whether you see this intellect or not, although you say it is of no importance. It appears to be of less importance than it really is, because I do not think that even you ever empty the universe of intellect. I believe that mind never worships anything but mind, and that you worship it when you admire the level bars of cloud over the setting sun. You think you eject mind, but you do not. I can only half imagine a belief which looks upon the world as a mindless blank, and if I could imagine it, it would be depressing in the last degree to me. I know that I have mind, and to live in a universe in which my mind is answered by no other would be unbearable. Better any sort of intelligence than none at all. But, as I have just said, your case admits of plainer statement than mine. You and I have talked this matter over before, and I have never gained a logical victory over you. Often I have felt thoroughly prostrated by you, and yet when I have left you the old superstition has arisen unsubdued. I do not know how it is, but I always feel that upon this, as upon many other subjects, I never can really speak myself. An unshapen thought presents itself to me, I look at it, and I do all in my power to give it body and expression, but I cannot. I am certain that there is something truer and deeper to be said about the existence of God than anything I have said, and what is more, I am certain of the presence of this something in me, but I cannot lift it to the light.'

'Ah, you are now getting into the region of sentiment, and I am unable to accompany you. When my friends go into the cloud, I never try to follow them.'

All this time Mary had been sitting in the armchair against the fireplace in her usual attitude, resting her head on her hand and with her feet crossed one over the other on the fender. She had been listening silently and motionless. She now closed her eyes and said—

'Father, father, it is not true.'

'What is not true?'

'I do not mean that what you have said about

theology is not true, but you make Mr. Rutherford believe you are what you are not. Mr.
Rutherford, father sometimes tells us he has no
sentiment, but you must take no notice of him
when he talks in that way. I always think of our
visit to the seaside two years ago. The railway
station was in a disagreeable part of the town, and
when we came out we walked along a dismal row
of very plain-looking houses. There were cards
in the window with "Lodgings" written on them,
and father wanted to go in to ask the terms. I
said that I did not wish to stay in such a dull
street, but father could not afford to pay for a
sea view, and so we went in to inquire. We then
found that what we thought were the fronts of the
houses were the backs, and that the fronts faced
the bay. They had pretty gardens on the other
side, and a glorious sunny prospect over the ocean.'

Mardon laughed and said—

'Ah, Mary, there is no sea-front here, and no
garden.'

I took up my hat and said I must go. Both
pressed me to stop, but I declined. Mardon urged
me again, and at last said—

'I believe you've never once heard Mary sing.'

Mary protested, and pleaded that as they had
no piano, Mr. Rutherford would not care for her
poor voice without any accompaniment. But I,
too, protested that I should, and she got out the
'Messiah.' Her father took a tuning-fork out of

his pocket, and having struck it, Mary rose and began, 'He was despised.'* Her voice was not powerful, but it was pure and clear, and she sang with that perfect taste which is begotten solely of a desire to honour the master. The song always had a profound charm for me. Partly this was due to association. The words and tones, which have been used to embody their emotions by those whom we have loved, are doubly expressive when we use them to embody our own. The song is potent too, because with utmost musical tenderness and strength, it reveals the secret of the influence of the story of Jesus. Nobody would be bold enough to cry, *That too is my case*, and yet the poorest and the humblest soul has a right to the consolation that Jesus was a man of sorrows and acquainted with grief. For some reason or the other, or for many reasons, Mary's voice wound itself into the very centre of my existence. I seemed to be listening to the tragedy of all human worth and genius. The ball rose in my throat, the tears mounted to my eyes, and I had to suppress myself rigidly. Presently she ceased. There was silence for a moment. I looked round, and saw that Mardon's face was on the table, buried in his hands. I felt that I had better go, for the presence of a stranger, when the heart is deeply stirred, is an intrusion. I noiselessly left the room, and Mary followed. When we got to the door she said: 'I forgot that mother used to sing that song. I ought to have known better.' Her own eyes were full; I thought the pressure of her hand as she bade me good-bye was a little firmer than usual, and as we parted an over-mastering impulse seized me. I lifted her hand to my lips; without giving her time to withdraw it, I gave it one burning kiss, and passed out into the street. It was pouring with rain, and I had neither overcoat nor umbrella, but I heeded not the heavens, and not till I got home to my own fireless, dark, solitary lodgings, did I become aware of any contrast between the sphere into which I had been exalted and the earthly commonplace world by which I was surrounded.

CHAPTER VII

EMANCIPATION

THE old Presbyterian chapels throughout the country have many of them become Unitarian*, and occasionally, even in an agricultural village, a respectable red brick building may be seen, dating from the time of Queen Anne, in which a few descendants of the eighteenth century heretics still testify against three Gods in one and the deity of Jesus Christ. Generally speaking, the attendance in these chapels is very meagre, but they are often endowed, and so they are kept open. There was one in the large straggling half-village, half-town of D——, within about ten miles of me, and the pulpit was then vacant. The income was about £100 a year. The principal man there was a small general dealer, who kept a shop in the middle of the village street, and I had come to know him slightly, because I had undertaken to give his boy a few lessons to prepare him for admission to a boarding-school. The money in my pocket was coming to an end, and as I did not suppose that any dishonesty would be imposed on me, and although the prospect was not cheering, I expressed my willingness to be considered as a candidate. In the course of a week or two I was therefore invited to preach. I was so reduced that I was obliged to walk the whole distance on the

Sunday morning, and as I was asked to no house, I went straight to the chapel, and loitered about in the graveyard till a woman came and opened a door at the back. I explained who I was, and sat down in a Windsor chair against a small kitchen table in the vestry. It was cold, but there was no fire, nor were any preparations made for one. On the mantel-shelf were a bottle of water and a glass, but as the water had evidently been there for some time, it was not very tempting. I waited in silence for about twenty minutes, and my friend the dealer then came in, and having shaken hands and remarked that it was chilly, asked me for the hymns. These I gave him and went into the pulpit. I found myself in a plain-looking building designed to hold about two hundred people. There was a gallery opposite me, and the floor was occupied with high, dark, brown pews, one or two immediately on my right and left being surrounded with faded green curtains. I counted my hearers, and discovered that there were exactly seventeen, including two very old labourers, who sat on a form near the door. The gallery was quite empty, except a little organ or seraphine, I think it was called, which was played by a young woman. The dealer gave out the hymns, and accompanied the seraphine in a bass voice, singing the air. A weak whisper might be perceived from the rest of the congregation, but nothing more. I was somewhat taken aback at finding in the Bible a discourse which had been left by one of my predecessors. It was a funeral sermon, neatly written, and had evidently done duty on several occasions, although the allusions in it might be considered personal. The piety and good works of the departed were praised with emphasis, but the masculine pronouns originally used were altered above the lines all throughout to feminine pronouns, and the word 'brother' to 'sister,' so that no difficulty might arise in reading it for either sex. I was faint, benumbed, and with no heart for anything. I talked for about half-an-hour about what I considered to be the real meaning of the death of Christ, thinking that this was a subject which might prove as attractive as any other. After the service the assembly of seventeen departed, save one thin elderly gentleman, who came into the vestry, and having made a slight bow, said: 'Mr. Rutherford, will you come with me, if you please?' I accordingly followed him, almost in silence, through the village till we reached his house, where his wife, who had gone on before, received us. They had formerly kept the shop which the dealer now had, but had retired. They might both be about sixty-five, and were of about the same temperament, pale, thin, and ineffectual, as if they had been fed on gruel. We had dinner in a large room with an old-fashioned grate in it, in which was stuck a basket stove. I remember perfectly well what we had for dinner. There was a neck of mutton (cold), potatoes, cabbage, a suet pudding, and some of the strangest-looking ale I ever saw—about the colour of lemon juice, but what it was really like I do not know, as I did not drink beer. I was somewhat surprised at being asked whether I would take potatoes *or* cabbage, but thinking it was the custom of the country not to indulge in both at once, and remembering that I was on probation, I said 'cabbage.' Very little was spoken during dinner-time by anybody, and scarcely a word by my hostess. After dinner she cleared the things away, and did not again appear. My host drew near the basket stove, and having remarked that it was beginning to rain, fell into a slumber. At twenty minutes to two we sallied out for the afternoon service, and found the seventeen again in their places, excepting the two labourers, who were probably prevented by the wet from attending. The service was a repetition of that in the morning, and when I came down my host again came forward and presented me with nineteen shillings. The fee was a guinea, but from that two shillings were abated for my entertainment. He informed me at the same time that a farmer, who had been hearing me and who lived five miles on my road, would give me a lift. He was a very large, stout man, with a rosy countenance, which was somewhat of a relief after the gruel face of my former friend. We went round to a stable-yard,

and I got into a four-wheeled chaise. His wife
sat with him in front, and a biggish boy sat with
me behind. When we came to the guide-post
which pointed down his lane, I got out, and was
dismissed in the dark with the observation—
uttered good-naturedly and jovially, but not very
helpfully—that he was 'afraid I should have a
wettish walk.' The walk certainly was wettish,
and as I had had nothing to eat or drink since my
midday meal, I was miserable and desponding.
But just before I reached home the clouds rolled
off with the south-west wind into detached, fleecy
masses, separated by liquid blue gulfs, in which
were sowed the stars, and the effect upon me was
what that sight, thank God, always has been—a
sense of the infinite, extinguishing all mean cares.

I expected to hear no more from my Unitarian
acquaintances, and was therefore greatly surprised when, a week after my visit, I received an
invitation to 'settle' amongst them. The usual
month's trial was thought unnecessary, as I was
not altogether a stranger to some of them. I
hardly knew what to do. I could not feel any
enthusiasm at the prospect of the engagement,
but, on the other hand, there was nothing else
before me. There is no more helpless person in
this world than a minister who is thrown out of
work. At any rate, I should be doing no harm if
I went. I pondered over the matter a good deal,
and then reflected that in a case where every

opening is barred save one, it is our duty not to plunge at an impassable barrier, but to take that one opening, however unpromising it may be. Accordingly I accepted. My income was to be a hundred a year, and it was proposed that I should lodge with my friend the retired dealer, who had the only two rooms in the village which were available. I went to bid Mardon and Mary good-bye. I had not seen either of them since the night of the song. To my surprise I found them both away. The blinds were down and the door locked. A neighbour, who heard me knocking, came out and told me the news. Mardon had had a dispute with his employer, and had gone to London to look for work. Mary had gone to see a relative at some distance, and would remain there until her father had determined what was to be done. I obtained the addresses of both of them, and wrote to Mardon, telling him what my destiny for the present was to be. To Mary I wrote also and to her I offered my heart. Looking backward, I have sometimes wondered that I felt so little hesitation; not that I have ever doubted since, that what I did then was the one perfectly right thing which I have done in my life, but because it was my habit so to confuse myself with meditative indecision. I had doubted before. I remember once being so near engaging myself to a girl that the desk was open and the paper under my hand. But I held back, could not make up my mind, and happily was stayed. Had I not been restrained, I should for ever have been miserable. The remembrance of this escape, and the certain knowledge that of all beings whom I knew I was most likely to be mistaken in an emergency, always produced in me a torturing tendency to inaction. There was no such tendency now. I thought I chose Mary, but there was no choice. The feeblest steel filing which is drawn to a magnet, would think, if it had consciousness, that it went to the magnet of its own free will. My soul rushed to hers as if dragged by the force of a loadstone.* But she was not to be mine. I had a note from her, a sweet note, thanking me with much tenderness for my affectionate regard for her, but saying that her mind had long since been made up. She was an only child of a mother whom her father had loved above everything in life, and she could never leave him nor suffer any affection to interfere with that which she felt for him and which he felt for her. I might well misinterpret him, and think it strange that he should be so much bound up in her. Few people knew him as she did.

The shock to me at first was overpowering, and I fell under the influence of that horrible monomania from which I had been free for so long. For weeks I was prostrate, with no power of resistance; the evil being intensified by my solitude. Of all the dreadful trials which human nature has the capacity to bear unshattered, the worst—as, indeed, I have already said—is the fang of some monomaniacal idea which cannot be wrenched out. A main part of the misery, as I have also said, lies in the belief that suffering of this kind is peculiar to ourselves. We are afraid to speak of it, and not knowing, therefore, how common it is, we are distracted with the fear that it is our own special disease. I managed to get through my duties, but how I cannot tell. Fortunately our calamities are not what they appear to be when they lie in perspective behind us or before us, for they actually consist of distinct moments, each of which is overcome by itself. I was helped by remembering my recovery before, and I was able now, as a reward of long-continued abstinence from wine, to lie much stiller, and wait with more patience till the cloud should lift. Mardon having gone to London, I was more alone than ever, but my love for Mary increased in intensity, and had a good deal to do with my restoration to health. It was a hopeless love, but to be in love hopelessly is more akin to sanity than careless, melancholy indifference to the world. I was relieved from myself by the anchorage of all my thoughts else-where. The pain of loss was great, but the main curse of my existence has not been pain or loss, but gloom; blind wandering in a world of black fog, haunted by apparitions. I am not going to expand upon the history of my silent relationship to Mary during that time. How can I? All that I felt has been described better by others; and if it had not been, I have no mind to attempt a description myself, which would answer no purpose. I continued to correspond with Mardon, but with Mary I interchanged no word. After her denial of me I should have dreaded the charge of selfishness if I had opened my lips again. I could not place myself in her affection before her father.

My work at the chapel was of the most lifeless kind. My people really consisted of five families— those of the retired dealer, the farmer who took me home the first day I preached, and a man who kept a shop in the village for the sale of all descriptions of goods, including ready-made clothing and provisions. He had a wife and one child. Then there was a superannuated brassfounder, who had a large house near, and who nominally was a Unitarian, having professed himself a Unitarian in the town in which he was formerly in business, where Unitarianism was flourishing. He had come down here to cultivate, for amusement, a few acres of ground, and play the squire at a cheap rate. Released from active employment, he had given himself over to eating and drinking, particularly the drinking of port wine. His wife was dead, his sons were in business for themselves, and his daughters all went to church. His connection with the chapel was merely nominal, and I was very glad it was so. I was hardly ever brought into contact with him, except as trustee, and once I was asked to his house to dinner; but the attempt to make me feel my inferiority was so painful, and the rudeness of his children was so marked, that I never went again. There was also a school-master, who kept a low-priced boarding-school with a Unitarian connection. He lived, however, at such a distance that his visits were very unfrequent. Sometimes on a fine summer's Sunday morning the boys would walk over—about twenty of them altogether, but this only happened perhaps half-a-dozen times in a year. Although my congregation had a freethought lineage, I do not think that I ever had anything to do with a more petrified set. With one exception, they were meagre in the extreme. They were perfectly orthodox, except that they denied a few ortho-dox doctrines. Their method was as strict as that of the most rigid Calvinist. They plumed themselves, however, greatly on their intellectual superiority over the Wesleyans*and Baptists round them; and so far as I could make out, the only topics they delighted in, were demonstrations of the unity of God from texts in the Bible, and polemics against tri-theism. Sympathy with the great problems then beginning to agitate men, they had none. Socially they were cold, and the entertainment at their houses was pale and pen-urious. They never considered themselves bound

to contribute a shilling to my support. There was
an endowment of a hundred a year, and they were
relieved from all further anxiety. They had no
enthusiasm for their chapel, and came or stayed
away on the Sunday just as it suited them, and
without caring to assign any reason. The one
exception was the wife of the shopkeeper. She
was a contrast to her husband and all the rest.
I do not think she was a Unitarian born and bred.
She talked but little about theology, but she was
devoted to her Bible, and had a fine sense for all
the passages in it which had an experience in
them. She was generous, spiritual, and possessed
of an unswerving instinct for what was right.
Oftentimes her prompt decisions were a scandal
to her more sedate friends, who did not believe
in any way of arriving at the truth except by
rationalising, but she hardly ever failed to hit the
mark. It was in questions of relationship between
persons, of behaviour, and of morals, that her
guidance was the surest. In such cases her force
seemed to keep her straight, while the weakness
of those around made it impossible for them not
to wander, first on one side and then on the other.
She was unflinching in her expressions, and at any
sacrifice did her duty. It was her severity in obey-
ing her conscience which not only gave authority
to her admonitions, but was the source of her in-
spirations. She was not much of a reader, but she
read strange things. She had some old volumes

of a magazine, a 'Repository' of some kind—I have forgotten what, and she picked out from them some translations of German verses which she greatly admired. She was not a well-educated woman in the school sense of the word, and of several of our greatest names in literature had heard nothing. I do not think she knew anything about Shakespeare, and she never entered into the meaning of dramatic poetry. At all points her path was her own, intersecting at every conceivable angle the paths of her acquaintances, and never straying along them, except just so far as they might happen to be hers. While I was in the village an event happened which caused much commotion. Her son was serving in the shop, and there was in the house at the time a nice-looking, clean servant-girl. Mrs. Lane, for that was my friend's name, had meditated discharging her, for, with her usual quickness, she thought she saw something in the behaviour of her son to the girl which was peculiar. One morning, however, both her son and the girl were absent, and there was a letter upon the table announcing that they were in a town about twenty miles off and were married. The shock was great, and a tumult of voices arose, confusing counsel. Mrs. Lane said but little, but never wavered an instant. Leaving her husband to 'consider what was best to be done,' she got out the gig, drove herself over to her son's lodging, and presented herself to her amazed

daughter-in-law, who fell upon her knees and
prayed for pity. 'My dear,' said Mrs. Lane, 'get
up this instant; you are my daughter. Not another word. I've come to see what you want.'
And she kissed her tenderly. The girl was at heart
a good girl. She was so bound to her late mistress
and her new mother by this behaviour, that the
very depths in her opened, and she loved Mrs.
Lane ever afterwards with almost religious fer-
vour. She was taught a little up to her son's level,
and a happier marriage I never knew. Mrs. Lane
told me what she had done, but she had no theory
about it. She merely said that she knew it to be
the right thing to do. She was very fond of getting
up early in the morning and going out, and in
such a village this was an eccentricity bordering
almost on lunacy. At five o'clock she was often
wandering about in her large garden. She was
a great lover of order in the house, and kept it
well under control, but I do not think I ever surprised her when she was so busy that she would
not easily, and without any apparent sacrifice,
leave what she was doing to come and talk with
me. As I have said, the world of books in which
I lived was almost altogether shut to her, but yet
she was the only person in the village whose conversation was lifted out of the petty and personal
into the region of the universal. I have been
thus particular in describing her—I fear without
raising any image of her—because she was of

incalculable service to me. I languished from lack of life, and her mere presence, so exuberant in its full vivacity, was like mountain air. Furthermore, she was not troubled much with my philosophical difficulties. They had not come in her path. Her world was the world of men and women—more particularly of those she knew, and it was a world in which it did me good to dwell. She was all the more important to me, because outside our own little circle there was no society whatever. The Church and the other dissenting bodies considered us as non-Christian. I often wondered that Mr. Lane retained his business, and, indeed, he would have lost it if he had not established a reputation for honesty, which drew customers to him, who, notwithstanding the denunciations of the parson, preferred tea with some taste in it from a Unitarian to the insipid wood-flavoured stuff which was sold by the grocer who believed in the Trinity.

CHAPTER VIII
PROGRESS IN EMANCIPATION

I WAS with my Unitarian congregation for about a twelvemonth. My life during that time, save so far as my intercourse with Mrs. Lane, and one other friend presently to be mentioned, was concerned, was as sunless and joyless as it had ever been. Imagine me living by myself, roaming about the fields, and absorbed mostly upon insoluble problems with which I never made any progress, and which tended to draw me away from what enjoyment of life there was which I might have had. One day I was walking along under the south side of a hill, which was a great place for butterflies, and I saw a man, apparently about fifty years old, coming along with a butterfly net.* He did not see me, for he looked about for a convenient piece of turf, and presently sat down, taking out a sandwich box, from which he produced his lunch. His occupation did not particularly attract me, but in those days, if I encountered a new person who was not repulsive, I was always as eager to make his acquaintance as if he perchance might solve a secret for me, the answer to which I burned to know. I have been disappointed so many times, and have found that nobody has much more to tell me, that my curiosity has somewhat abated, but even now, the news that anybody who has the reputation for intelligence has come near me, makes me restless to see him. I accordingly saluted the butterfly catcher, who returned the salutation kindly, and we began to talk. He told me that he had come seven miles that morning to that spot, because he knew that it was haunted by one particular species of butterfly which he wished to get; and as it was a still, bright day, he hoped to find a specimen. He had been unsuccessful for some years. Presupposing that I knew all about his science, he began to discourse upon it with great freedom, and he ended by saying that he would be happy to show me his collection, which was one of the finest in the country.

'But I forget,' said he, 'as I always forget in such cases, perhaps you don't care for butterflies.'

'I take much interest in them. I admire exceedingly the beauty of their colours.'

'Ah, yes, but you don't care for them scientifically, or for collecting them.'

'No, not particularly. I cannot say I ever saw much pleasure in the mere classification of insects.'

'Perhaps you are devoted to some other science?'

'No, I am not.'

'Well, I daresay it looks absurd for a man at my years to be running after a moth. I used to think it was absurd, but I am wiser now. However, I cannot stop to talk; I shall lose the sunshine. The first time you are anywhere near me, come and have a look. You will alter your opinion.'

Some weeks afterwards I happened to be in the neighbourhood of the butterfly catcher's house, and I called. He was at home, and welcomed me cordially. The first thing he did was to show me his little museum. It was really a wonderful exhibition, and as I saw the creatures in lines, and noted the amazing variations of the single type, I was filled with astonishment. Seeing the butterflies systematically arranged was a totally different thing from seeing a butterfly here and there, and gave rise to altogether new thoughts. My friend knew his subject from end to end, and I envied him his mastery of it. I had often craved the mastery of some one particular province, be it ever so minute. I half or a quarter knew a multitude of things, but no one thing thoroughly, and was never sure, just when I most wanted to be sure. We got into conversation, and I was urged to stay to dinner. I consented, and found that my friend's household consisted of himself alone. After dinner, as we became a little more communicative, I asked him when and how he took to this pursuit.

'It will be twenty-six years ago next Christmas,' said he, 'since I suffered a great calamity. You will forgive my saying anything about it, as I have no assurance that the wound which looks healed may not break out again. Suffice to say, that for some ten years or more my thoughts were almost entirely occupied with death and our future state. There is a strange fascination about these topics to many people, because they are topics which permit a great deal of dreaming, but very little thinking: in fact, true thinking, in the proper sense of the word, is impossible in dealing with them. There is no rigorous advance from one position to another, which is really all that makes thinking worth the name. Every man can imagine or say cloudy things about death and the future, and feel himself here, at least, on a level with the ablest brain which he knows. I went on gazing gloomily into dark emptiness, till all life became nothing for me. I did not care to live, because there was no assurance of existence beyond. By the strangest of processes, I neglected the world, because I had so short a time to be in it. It is with absolute horror now that I look back upon those days, when I lay as if alive in a coffin of lead. All passions and pursuits were nullified by the ever-abiding sense of mortality. For years this mood endured, and I was near being brought down to the very dust. At last, by the greatest piece of good fortune, I was obliged to go abroad. The change, and the obligation to occupy myself about many affairs, was an incalculable blessing to me. While travelling I was struck with the remarkable and tropical beauty of the insects, and especially of the butterflies. I captured a few, and brought them home. On showing them to a friend, learned in such matters, I discovered that they were rare, and I had a little cabinet made for them. I looked into the books, found what it was which I had got, and what I had not got. Next year it was my duty to go abroad again, and I went with some feeling akin to pleasure, for I wished to add to my store. I increased it considerably, and by the time I returned I had as fine a show as any private person might wish to possess. A good deal of my satisfaction, perhaps, was unaccountable, and no rational explanation can be given of it. But men should not be too curious in analysing and condemning any means which nature devises to save them from themselves, whether it be coins, old books, curiosities, butterflies, or fossils. And yet my newly-acquired passion was not altogether inexplicable. I was the owner of something which other persons did not own, and in a little while, in my own limited domain I was supreme. No man either can study any particular science thoroughly without transcending it; and it is an utter mistake to suppose, that because a student sticks to any one branch, he necessarily becomes contracted. However, I am not going to philosophise; I do not like it. All I can say is, that I shun all those metaphysical speculations of former years as I would a path which leads to madness. Other people may be able to occupy themselves with them and be happy; I cannot. I find quite enough in my butterflies to exercise my wonder, and yet, on the other hand, my study is not a mere vacant, profit-less stare. When you saw me that morning, I was trying to obtain an example which I have long wanted to fill up a gap. I have looked for it for years, but have missed it. But I know it has been seen lately where we met, and I shall triumph at last.'

A good deal of all this was to me incomprehens-ible. It seemed mere solemn trifling compared with the investigation of those great questions with which I had been occupied, but I could not resist the contagion of my friend's enthusiasm when he took me to his little library, and identi-fied his treasures with pride, pointing out at the same time those in which he was deficient. He was specially exultant over one minute creature which he had caught himself, which he had not as yet seen figured, and he proposed going to the British Museum almost on purpose to see if he could find it there.

When I got home I made inquiries into the his-tory of my entomologist. I found that years ago he had married a delicate girl, of whom he was devotedly fond. She died in childbirth, leaving him completely broken. Her offspring, a boy, survived, but he was a cripple, and grew up deformed. As he neared manhood he developed a satyr-like lustfulness, which was almost uncon-

trollable, and made it difficult to keep him at
home without constraint. He seemed to have no
natural affection for his father, nor for anybody
else, but was cunning with the base beastly cunning of the ape. The father's horror was infinite.
This thing was his only child, and the child of the
woman whom he worshipped. He was excluded
from all intercourse with friends; for, as the boy
could not be said to be mad, he could not be shut
up. After years of inconceivable misery, however,
lust did deepen into absolute lunacy, and the
crooked, mis-shapen monster was carried off to an
asylum, where he died, and the father well-nigh
went there too.

Before I had been six months amongst the Unitarians, I found life even more intolerable with
them than it had been with the Independents.
The difference of a little less belief was nothing.
The question of Unitarianism was altogether dead
to me; and although there was a phase of the
doctrine of God's unity which would now and then
give me an opportunity for a few words which I
felt, it was not a phase for which my hearers in
the least cared or which they understood. Here,
as amongst the Independents, there was the same
lack of personal affection, or even of a capability
of it—excepting always Mrs. Lane—and, in fact,
it was more distressing amongst the Unitarians
than amongst the orthodox. The desire for something like sympathy and love absolutely devoured

me. I dwelt on all the instances in poetry and history in which one human being had been bound to another human being, and I reflected that my existence was of no earthly importance to anybody. I could not altogether lay the blame on myself. God knows that I would have stood against a wall and have been shot for any man or woman whom I loved, as cheerfully as I would have gone to bed, but nobody seemed to wish for such a love, or to know what to do with it. Oh the humiliations under which this weakness has bent me! Often and often I have thought that I have discovered somebody who could really comprehend the value of a passion which could tell everything and venture everything. I have overstepped all bounds of etiquette in obtruding myself on him, and have opened my heart even to shame. I have then found that it was all on my side. For every dozen times I went to his house, he came to mine once, and only when pressed: I have languished in sickness for a month without his finding it out; and if I were to drop into the grave, he would perhaps never give me another thought. If I had been born a hundred years earlier, I should have transferred this burning longing to the unseen God and have become a devotee. But I was a hundred years too late, and I felt that it was mere cheating of myself and a mockery to think about love for the only God whom I knew, the forces which maintained the universe. I am now getting old, and have altered in many things. The hunger and thirst of those years have abated, or rather, the fire has had ashes heaped on it, so that it is well-nigh extinguished. I have been repulsed into self-reliance and reserve, having learned wisdom by experience; but still I know that the desire has not died, as so many other desires have died, by the natural evolution of age. It has been forcibly suppressed, and that is all. If anybody who reads these words of mine should be offered by any young dreamer such a devotion as I once had to offer, and had to take back again refused so often, let him in the name of all that is sacred accept it. It is simply the most precious thing in existence. Had I found anybody who would have thought so, my life would have been redeemed into something which I have often imagined, but now shall never know.

I determined to leave, but what to do I could not tell. I was fit for nothing, and yet I could not make up my mind to accept a life which was simply living. It must be a life through which some benefit was conferred upon my fellow-creatures. This was mainly delusion. I had not then learned to correct this natural instinct to be of some service to mankind by the thought of the boundlessness of infinity and of nature's profuseness. I had not come to reflect that, taking into account her eternities, and absolute exhaustlessness, it was folly in me to fret and fume, and I therefore clung to the hope that I might employ myself in some way which, however feebly, would help mankind a little to the realisation of an ideal. But I was not the man for such a mission. I lacked altogether that concentration which binds up the scattered powers into one resistless energy, and I lacked faith. All I could do was to play the vagrant in literature, picking up here and there an idea which attracted me, and presenting it to my flock on the Sunday; the net result being next to nothing. However, existence like that which I had been leading was intolerable, and change it I must. I accordingly resigned, and with ten pounds in my pocket, which was all that remained after paying my bills, I came to London, thinking that until I could settle what to do, I would try and teach in a school. I called on an agent somewhere near the Strand, and after a little negotiation, was engaged by a gentleman who kept a private establishment at Stoke Newington.* Thither I accordingly went one Monday afternoon in January, about two days before the term commenced. When I got there, I was shown into a long schoolroom, which had been built out from the main building. It was dark, save for one candle, and was warmed by a stove. The walls were partly covered with maps, and at one end of the room hung a diagram representing a globe, on which an immense amount of wasted ingenuity had been spent to produce the illusion of solidity.

The master, I was told, was out, and in this room
with one candle I remained till nine o'clock. At
that time a servant brought me some bread and
cheese on a small tray, with half-a-pint of beer.
I asked for water, which was given me, and she
then retired. The tray was set down on the
master's raised desk, and sitting there I ate my
supper in silence, looking down upon the dimly-
lighted forms, and forward into the almost absolute gloom. At ten o'clock a man, who seemed as
if he were the knife and boot cleaner, came and
said he would show me where I was to sleep. We
passed through the schoolroom into a kind of
court, where there was a ladder standing against
a trap-door. He told me that my bedroom was
up there, and that when I got up I could leave
the ladder down, or pull it up after me, just
as I pleased. I ascended and found a little chamber, duly furnished with a chest of drawers, bed,
and washhand stand. It was tolerably clean and
decent; but who shall describe what I felt. I went
to the window and looked out. There were scattered lights here and there marking roads, but as
they crossed one another, and now and then
stopped where building had ceased, the effect
they produced was that of bewilderment with no
clue to it. Further off was the great light of London, like some unnatural dawn, or the illumination from a fire which could not itself be seen.
I was overcome with the most dreadful sense of

loneliness. I suppose it is the very essence of passion, using the word in its literal sense, that no account can be given of it by the reason. Reflecting on what I suffered then, I cannot find any solid ground for it, and yet there are not half-a-dozen days or nights of my life which remain with me like that one. I was beside myself with a kind of terror, which I cannot further explain. It is possible for another person to understand grief for the death of a friend, bodily suffering, or any emotion which has a distinct cause, but how shall he understand the worst of all calamities, the nameless dread, the efflux of all vitality, the ghostly haunting horror which is so nearly akin to madness? It is many years ago since that evening, but while I write I am at the window still, and the yellow flare of the city is still in my eyes. I remember the thought of all the happy homes which lay around me, in which dwelt men who had found a position, an occupation, and, above all things, affection. I know the causelessness of a good deal of all those panic fears, and all that suffering, but I tremble to think how thin is the floor on which we stand which separates us from the bottomless abyss.

The next morning I went down into the school-room, and after I had been there for some little time, the proprietor of the school made his appearance. He was not a bad man, nor even unkind in his way, but he was utterly uninteresting, and as

commonplace as might be expected after having
for many years done nothing but fight a very
uphill battle in boarding the sons of tradesfolk,
and teaching them, at very moderate rates, the
elements of Latin, and the various branches of
learning which constitute what is called a commercial education. He said that he expected some
of the boys back that day; that when they came,
he should wish me to take my meals with them,
but that meanwhile he would be glad if I would
breakfast with him and his wife. This accordingly
I did. What his wife was like I have almost
entirely forgotten, and I only saw her once again.
After breakfast he said I could go for a walk,
and for a walk I went; wandering about the
dreary intermingled chaos of fields with damaged
hedges, and new roads divided into building
plots.

Meanwhile one or two of the boys had made
their appearance, and I therefore had my dinner
with them. After dinner, as there was nothing
particular to do, I was again dismissed with them
for a walk just as the light of the winter afternoon
was fading. My companions were dejected, and
so was I. The wind was south-easterly, cold and
raw, and the smoke came up from the region about
the river and shrouded all the building plots in
fog. I was now something more than depressed.
It was absolutely impossible to endure such a
state of things any longer, and I determined that,

come what might, I would not stop. I considered whether I should leave without saying a word, that is to say, whether I should escape, but I feared pursuit and some unknown legal proceedings. When I got home, therefore, I sought the principal, and informed him that I felt so unwell that I was afraid I must throw up my engagement at once. He naturally observed that this was a serious business for him; that my decision was very hasty—what was the matter with me? I might get better; but he concluded, after my reiterated asseverations that I must go, with a permission to resign, only on one condition, that I should obtain an equally efficient substitute at the same salary. I was more agitated than ever. With my natural tendency to believe the worst, I had not the least expectation of finding anybody who would release me. The next morning I departed on my errand. I knew a poor student who had been at college with me, and who had nothing to do, and to him I betook myself. I strove—as even now I firmly believe—not to make the situation seem any better than it was, and he consented to take it. I have no clear recollection of anything that happened till the following day, excepting that I remember with all the vividness of actual and present sensuous perception, lugging my box down the ladder and sending for a cab. I was in a fever lest anything should arrest me, but the cab came, and I departed. When I had got fairly clear of the gates, I literally cried tears of joy—the first and the last of my life. I am constrained now, however, to admit that my trouble was but a bubble blown of air, and I doubt whether I have done any good by dwelling upon it.

CHAPTER IX

OXFORD STREET

Until I had actually left, I hardly knew where I was going, but at last I made up my mind I would go to Reuben Shapcott, another fellow-student, whom I knew to be living in lodgings in one of the streets just then beginning to creep over the unoccupied ground between Camden Town and Haverstock Hill, near the Chalk Farm turn-pike gate. To his address I betook myself, and found him not at home. He, like me, had been unsuccessful as a minister, and wrote a London letter for two country papers, making up about £100 or £120 a year by preaching occasionally in small Unitarian chapels in the country. I waited till his return, and told him my story. He advised me to take a bed in the house where he was stay-ing, and to consider what could be done. At first I thought I would consult Mardon, but I could not bring myself to go near him. How was I to behave in Mary's presence? During the last few months she had been so continually before me, that it would have been absolutely impossible for me to treat her with assumed indifference. I could not have trusted myself to attempt it. When I had been lying alone and awake at night, I had thought of all the endless miles of hill and valley that lay outside my window, separating me from the one house in which I could be at peace; and at times I scarcely prevented myself from getting up and taking the mail train and presenting myself at Mardon's door, braving all consequences. With the morning light, however, would come cooler thoughts, and a dull sense of impossibility. This, I know, was not pure love for her; it was a selfish passion for relief. But then I have never known what is meant by a perfectly pure love. When Christian was in the Valley of the Shadow of Death, and, being brought to the mouth of hell, was forced to put up his sword, and could do no other than cry, *O Lord, I beseech Thee, deliver my soul*, he heard a voice going before him and saying, *Though I walk through the Valley of the Shadow of Death, I will fear none ill, for Thou art with me*. And by and by the day broke. 'Then,' said Christian, 'He hath turned the Shadow of Death into morning. Whereupon Christian sang—

'Oh world of wonders! (I can say no less)
That I should be preserved in that distress
That I have met with here! Oh, blessed be
*That hand that from it hath delivered me!'**

This was Christian's love for God, and for God as his helper. Was that perfectly pure? However, this is a digression. I determined to help myself in my own way, and thought I would try the publishers. One morning I walked from Camden Town to Paternoster Row.* I went straightway into two or three shops and asked whether they wanted anybody. I was ready to do the ordinary work of a publisher's assistant, and aspired no higher. I met with several refusals, some of them not over polite, and the degradation—for so I felt it—of wandering through the streets and suing for employment cut me keenly. I remember one man in particular, who spoke to me with the mechanical brutality with which probably he replied to a score of similar applications every week. He sat in a little glass box at the end of a long dark room lighted with gas. It was a bitterly cold room, with no contrivance for warming it, but in his box there was a fire burning for his own special benefit. He surveyed all his clerks unceasingly, and woe betide the unhappy wretch who was caught idling. He and his slaves reminded me of the thrashing machine which is worked by horses walking round in a ring, the driver being perched on a high stool in the middle and armed with a long whip. While I was waiting his pleasure, he came out and spoke to one or two of his miserable subordinates words of directest and sharpest rebuke, without anger or the least loss of self-possession, and yet without the least attempt to mitigate their severity. I meditated much upon him. If ever I had occasion to rebuke anybody, I always did it apologetically, unless I happened to be in a flaming passion—and this was my habit, not from any respectable motive of consideration

for the person rebuked, but partly because I am
timid, and partly because I shrink from giving
pain. This man said with perfect ease what I
could not have said unless I had been wrought
up to white heat. With all my dislike to him, I
envied him: I envied his complete certainty; for
although his language was harsh in the extreme,
he was always sure of his ground, and the victim
upon whom his lash descended could never say
that he had given absolutely no reason for the
chastisement, and that it was altogether a mistake.
I envied also his ability to make himself disagreeable and care nothing about it; his power to walk
in his own path, and his resolve to succeed, no
matter what the cost might be. As I left him, it
occurred to me that I might be more successful
perhaps with a publisher of whom I had heard,
who published and sold books of a sceptical turn.
To him I accordingly went, and although I had
no introductions or recommendatory letters, I was
received, if not with a cordiality, at least with an
interest which surprised me. He took me into a
little back shop, and after hearing patiently what
I wanted, he asked me somewhat abruptly what
I thought of the miracles in the Bible. This was
a curious question if he wished to understand my
character; but his mind so constantly revolved in
one circle, and existed so completely by hostility
to the prevailing orthodoxy, that belief or disbelief
in it was the standard by which he judged men.

It was a very absurd standard doubtless, but no more absurd than many others, and not so absurd then as it would be now, when heresy is becoming more fashionable. I explained to him as well as I could what my position was; that I did not suppose that the miracles actually happened as they are recorded, but that, generally speaking, the miracle was a very intense statement of a divine truth; in fact, a truth which was felt with a more than common intensity seemed to take naturally a miraculous expression. Hence, so far from neglecting the miraculous stories of the Bible as simply outside me, I rejoiced in them, more, perhaps, than in the plain historical or didactic prose. He seemed content, although hardly to comprehend, and the result was that he asked me if I would help him in his business. In order to do this, it would be more economical if I would live in his house, which was too big for him. He promised to give me £40 a year, in addition to board and lodging. I joyously assented, and the bargain was struck. The next day I came to my new quarters. I found that he was a bachelor, with a niece, apparently about four or five and twenty years old, acting as a housekeeper, who assisted him in literary work. My own room was at the top of the house, warm, quiet, and comfortable, although the view was nothing but a wide reaching assemblage of chimney pots. My hours were long—from nine in the morning till seven in the evening; but this

I did not mind. I felt that if I was not happy, I was at least protected, and that I was with a man who cared for me, and for whom I cared. The first day I went there, he said that I could have a fire in my bedroom whenever I chose, so that I could always retreat to it when I wished to be by myself. As for my duties, I was to sell his books, keep his accounts, read proofs, run errands, and, in short, do just what he did himself. After my first morning's work we went upstairs to dinner, and I was introduced to 'my niece Theresa.'* I was rather surprised that I should have been admitted to a house in which there lived a young woman with no mother nor aunt, but this surprise ceased when I came to know more of Theresa and her uncle. She had yellowish hair which was naturally waved, a big arched head, greyish blue eyes, so far as I could make out, and a mouth which, although it had curves in it, was compressed and indicative of great force of character. She was rather short, with square shoulders, and she had a singularly vigorous firm walk. She had a way, when she was not eating or drinking, of sitting back in her chair at table and looking straight at the person with whom she was talking. Her uncle, whom, by the way, I had forgotten to name—his name was Wollaston—happened to know some popular preacher whom I knew, and I said that I wondered so many people went to hear him, for I believed him to be a hypocrite, and hypocrisy was one of the easiest of crimes to discover. Theresa, who had hitherto been silent, and was reclining in her usual attitude, instantly broke out with an emphasis and directness which quite startled me.

'The easiest to discover, do you think, Mr. Rutherford; I think it is the most difficult, at least for ordinary persons; and when they do discover it, I believe they like it, especially if it is successful. They like the sanction it gives to their own hypocrisy. They like a man to come to them who will say to them, "We are all hypocrites together," and who will put his finger to his nose and comfort them. Don't you think so yourself?'

In conversation I was always a bad hand at assuming a position contrary to the one assumed by the person to whom I might be talking; nor could I persistently maintain my own position if it happened to be opposed. I always rather tried to see as my opponent saw, and to discover how much there was in him with which I could sympathise. I therefore assented weakly to Theresa, and she seemed disappointed. Dinner was just over; she got up and rang the bell and went out of the room.

I found my work very hard, and some of it even loathsome. Particularly loathsome was that part of it which brought me into contact with the trade. I had to sell books to the booksellers' assistants,

and I had to collect books myself. These duties
are usually undertaken in large establishments by
men specially trained, who receive a low rate of
wages, and who are rather a rough set. It was
totally different work to anything I had ever had
to do before, and I suffered as a man with soft
hands would suffer, who was suddenly called to
be a blacksmith or a dock-labourer. Specially,
too, did I miss the country. London lay round
me like a mausoleum. I got into the habit of
rising very early in the morning and walking out
to Kensington Gardens and back before breakfast, varying my route occasionally so as even to
reach Battersea Bridge, which was always a favourite spot with me. Kensington Gardens and Battersea Bridge were poor substitutes for the downs,
and for the level stretch by the river towards the
sea where I first saw Mardon, but we make too
much of circumstances, and the very pressure of
London produced a sensibility to whatever loveliness could be apprehended there, which was
absent when loveliness was always around me.
The stars seen in Oxford Street late one night;
a sunset one summer evening from Lambeth pier;
and above everything, Piccadilly very early one
summer morning, abide with me still, when much
that was more romantic has been forgotten. On
the whole, I was not unhappy. The constant outward occupation prevented any eating of the heart
or undue brooding over problems which were

insoluble, at least for my intellect, and on that very
account fascinated me the more. I do not think
that Wollaston cared much for me personally. He
was a curious compound, materialistic yet impul-
sive, and for ever drawn to some new thing; without any love for anybody particularly, as far as I
could see, and yet with much more general kindness and philanthropy than many a man possess-
ing much stronger sympathies and antipathies.
There was no holy of holies*in him, into which one
or two of the elect could occasionally be admitted
and feel God to be there. He was no temple, but
rather a comfortable hospitable house open to all
friends, well furnished with books and pictures,
and free to every guest from garret to cellar. He
had 'liberal' notions about the relationship between the sexes. Not that he was a libertine, but
he disbelieved in marriage, excepting for so long
as husband and wife are a necessity to one another.
If one should find the other uninteresting, or
somebody else more interesting, he thought there
ought to be a separation. All this I soon learned
from him, for he was communicative without any
reserve. His treatment of his niece was peculiar.
He would talk on all kinds of subjects before her,
for he had a theory that she ought to receive precisely the same social training as men, and should
know just what men knew. He was never coarse,
but on the other hand he would say things to her
in my presence, which brought a flame into my

face. What the evil consequences of this might
be, I could not at once foresee, but one good result
obviously was, that in his house there was nothing
of that execrable practice of talking down to
women; there was no change of level when women
were present. One day he began to speak about
a novel which everybody was reading then, and
I happened to say that I wished people who wrote
novels would not write as if love were the very
centre and sum of human existence. A man's life
was made up of so much besides love, and yet
novelists were never weary of repeating the same
story, telling it over and over again in a hundred
different forms.

'I do not agree with you,' said Theresa. 'I dis-
agree with you utterly. I dislike foolish inane
sentiment—it makes me sick; but I do believe,
in the first place, that no man was ever good for
anything who has not been devoured, I was going
to say, by a great devotion to a woman. The
lives of your great men are as much the history
of women whom they adored as of themselves.
Dante, Byron, Shelley, it is the same with all of
them, and there is no mistake about it; it is the
great fact of life. What would Shakespeare be
without it? and Shakespeare *is* life. A man, worthy
to be named a man, will find the fact of love perpetually confronting him till he reaches old age,
and if he be not ruined by worldliness or dissipa-
tion, will be troubled by it when he is fifty as much

as when he was twenty-five. It is the subject of all subjects. People abuse love, and think it the cause of half the mischief in the world. It is the one thing that keeps the world straight, and if it were not for that overpowering instinct, human nature would fall asunder; would be the prey of inconceivable selfishness and vices, and finally, there would be universal suicide. I did not intend to be eloquent: I hate being eloquent. But you did not mean what you said; you spoke from the head or teeth merely.'

Theresa's little speech was delivered not with any heat of the blood. There was no excitement in her grey eyes, nor did her cheek burn. Her brain seemed to rule everything. This was an idea she had, and she kindled over it because it was an idea. It was impossible, of course, that she should say what she did without some movement of the organ in her breast, but how much share this organ had in her utterances, I never could make out. How much was due to the interest which she as a looker-on felt in men and women, and how much was due to herself as a woman, was always a mystery to me. She was fond of music, and occasionally I asked her to play to me. She had a great contempt for bungling, and not being a professional player, she never would try a piece in my presence of which she was not perfectly master. She particularly liked to play Mozart, and on my asking her once to play a piece of Beethoven, she turned round upon me and said: 'You like Beethoven best. I knew you would. He encourages a luxurious revelling in the incomprehensible and indefinably sublime. He is not good for you.'

My work was so hard, and the hours were so long, that I had little or no time for reading, nor for thinking either, except so far as Wollaston and Theresa made me think. Wollaston himself took rather to science, although he was not scientific, and made a good deal of what he called psychology. He was not very profound, but he had picked up a few phrases, or if this word is too harsh, a few ideas about metaphysical matters from authors who contemned metaphysics, and with these he was perfectly satisfied. A stranger listening to him would at first consider him well read, but would soon be undeceived, and would find that these ideas were acquired long ago; that he had never gone behind or below them, and that they had never fructified in him, but were like hard stones, which he rattled in his pocket. He was totally unlike Mardon. Mardon, although he would have agreed with many of Wollaston's results, differed entirely from him in the processes by which they had been brought about; and a mental comparison of the two often told me what I had been told over and over again, that what we believe is not of so much importance as the path by which we travel to it. Theresa too, like her uncle, eschewed metaphysics, but she was a woman, and a woman's impulses supplied in her the lack of those deeper questionings, and at times prompted them. She was far more original than he was, and was impatient of the narrowness of the circle in which he moved. Her love of music, for example, was a thing incomprehensible to him, and I do not remember that he ever sat for a quarter of an hour really listening to it. He would read the newspaper or do anything while she was playing. She never resented his inattention, except when he made a noise, and then, without any rebuke, she would break off and go away. This mode of treatment was the outcome of one of her theories. She disbelieved altogether in punishment, except when it was likely to do good, either to the person punished or to others. 'A good deal of punishment,' she used to say, 'is mere useless pain.'

Both Theresa and her uncle were kind and human, and I endeavoured to my utmost to repay them by working my hardest. My few hours of leisure were sweet, and when I spent them with Wollaston and Theresa, were interesting. I often asked myself why I found this mode of existence more tolerable than any other I had hitherto enjoyed. I had, it is true, an hour or two's unspeakable peace in the early morning, but, as I have said, at nine my toil commenced, and, with a very brief interval for meals, lasted

till seven. After seven I was too tired to do anything by myself, and could only keep awake if I
happened to be in company. One reason certainly
why I was content, was Theresa herself. She was
a constant study to me, and I could not for a long
time obtain any consistent idea of her. She was
not a this or a that or the other. She could not
be summarily dismissed into any ordinary classification. At first I was sure she was hard, but I
found by the merest accident that nearly all her
earnings were given with utmost secrecy to support a couple of poor relatives. Then I thought
her self-conscious, but this, when I came to think
upon it, seemed a mere word. She was one of
those women, and very rare they are, who deal in
ideas, and reflectiveness must be self-conscious.
At times she appeared passionless, so completely
did her intellect dominate, and so superior was
she to all the little arts and weaknesses of women;
but this was a criticism she contradicted continually. There was very little society at the Wollas-
tons', but occasionally a few friends called. One
evening there was a little party, and the conversation flagged. Theresa said that it was a great mistake to bring people together with nothing special
to do but talk. Nothing is more tedious than to
be in a company assembled for no particular
reason, and every host, if he asks more than two
persons at the outside, ought to provide some
entertainment. Talking is worth nothing unless

it is perfectly spontaneous, and it cannot be spontaneous if there are sudden and blank silences, and nobody can think of a fresh departure. The master of the house is bound to do something. He ought to hire a Punch and Judy show, or get up a dance. This spice of bitterness and flavour of rudeness was altogether characteristic of Theresa, and somebody resented it by reminding her that *she* was the hostess. 'Of course,' she replied, 'that is why I said it: what shall I do?' One of her gifts was memory, and her friends cried out at once that she should recite something. She hesitated a little, and then throwing herself back in her chair, began '*The Lass of Lochroyan*.'* At first she was rather diffident, but she gathered strength as she went on. There is a passage in the middle of the poem, in which Lord Gregory's cruel mother pretends she is Lord Gregory, and refuses to recognise his former love, Annie of Lochroyan, as she stands outside his tower. The mother calls to Annie from the inside

> '*Gin thou be Annie of Lochroyan*
>   (*As I trow thou binna she*),
> *Now tell me some of the love tokens*
>   *That passed between thee and me.*'

> '*Oh dinna ye mind, Lord Gregory,*
>   *As we sat at the wine,*
> *We changed the rings frae our fingers,*
>   *And I can show thee thine?*

> '*Oh yours was gude, and gude enough,*
> *But aye the best was mine;*
> *For yours was o' the gude red gowd,*
> But mine o' the diamond fine.'

The last verse is as noble as anything in any ballad in the English language, and I thought that when Theresa was half way through it her voice shook a good deal. There was a glass of flowers standing near her, and just as she came to an end her arm moved and the glass was in a moment on the floor, shivered into twenty pieces. I happened to be watching her and felt perfectly sure that the movement of her arm was not accidental, and that her intention was to conceal, by the apparent mishap, an emotion which was increasing and becoming inconvenient. At any rate, if that was her object it was perfectly accomplished, for the recitation was abruptly terminated, there was general commiseration over the shattered vase, and when the pieces were picked up and and order was restored, it was nearly time to separate.

Two of my chief failings*were forgetfulness and a want of thoroughness in investigation. What misery have I not suffered from insufficient presentation of a case to myself, and from prompt conviction of insufficiency and inaccuracy by the person to whom I in turn presented it! What misery have I not suffered from the discovery that explicit directions to me had been overlooked or only half understood! One day in particular, I had to take round a book to be 'subscribed' which Wollaston had just published, that is to say, I had to take a copy to each of the leading booksellers to see how many they would purchase. Some books are sold 'thirteen as twelve,' the thirteenth book being given to the purchaser of twelve, and some are sold 'twenty-five as twenty-four.' This book was to be sold 'twenty-five as twenty-four' according to Wollaston's orders. I subscribed it thirteen as twelve. Wollaston was annoyed, as I could see, for I had to go over all my work again, but in accordance with his fixed principles, he was not out of temper. It so happened that that same day he gave me some business correspondence which I was to look through; and having looked through it, I was to answer the last letter in the sense which he indicated. I read the correspondence and wrote the letter for his signature. As soon as he saw it, he pointed out to me that I had only half mastered the facts, and that my letter was all wrong. This greatly disturbed me, not only because I had vexed him and disappointed him, but because it was renewed evidence of my weakness. I thought that if I was incapable of getting to the bottom of such a very shallow complication as this, of what value were any of my thinkings on more difficult subjects, and I fell a prey to self-contempt and scepticism. Contempt from those about us is hard to bear, but God help the poor wretch who contemns himself. How well I recollect the early walk on the following morning in Kensington Gardens, the feeling of my own utter worthlessness, and the longing for death as the cancellation of the blunder of my existence! I went home, and after breakfast some proofs came from the printer of a pamphlet which Wollaston had in hand. Without unfastening them, he gave them to me, and said that as he had no time to read them himself, I must go upstairs to Theresa's study and read them off with her. Accordingly I went and began to read. She took the manuscript and I took the proof. She read about a page, and then she suddenly stopped. 'O Mr. Rutherford,' she said, 'what have you done? I heard my uncle distinctly tell you to mark on the manuscript, when it went to the printer, that it was to be printed in demy octavo, and you have marked it twelvemo.'* I had had little sleep that night, I was exhausted with my early walk, and suddenly the room seemed to fade from me and I fainted. When I came to myself, I found that Theresa had not sought for any help; she had done all that ought to be done. She had unfastened my collar and had sponged my face with cold water. The first thing I saw as I gradually recovered myself, was her eyes looking steadily at me as she stood over me, and I felt her hand upon my head. When she was sure I was coming to myself, she held off and sat down in her chair. I was a little hysterical, and after the fit was over I broke loose. With a storm of tears, I laid open all my heart. I told her how nothing I had ever attempted had succeeded; that I had never even been able to attain that degree of satisfaction with myself and my own conclusions, without which a man cannot live; and that now I found I was useless, even to the best friends I had ever known, and that the meanest clerk in the city would serve them better than I did. I was beside myself, and I threw myself on my knees, burying my face in Theresa's lap and sobbing convulsively. She did not repel me, but she gently passed her fingers through my hair. Oh the transport of that touch! It was as if water had been poured on a burnt hand, or some miraculous Messiah had soothed the delirium of a fever-striken sufferer, and replaced his visions of torment with dreams of Paradise. She gently lifted me up, and as I rose I saw her eyes too were wet. 'My poor friend,' she said, 'I cannot talk to you now. You are not strong enough, and for that matter, nor am I, but let me say this to you, that you are altogether mistaken about yourself. The meanest clerk in the city could not take your place here.' There was just a slight emphasis I thought upon the word 'here.' 'Now,' she said, 'you had better go. I will see about the pamphlet.' I went out mechanically, and I anticipate my story so far as to say that, two days after, another proof came in the proper form. I went to the printer to offer to pay for setting it up afresh, and was told that Miss Wollaston had been there and had paid herself for the rectification of the mistake, giving special injunctions that no notice of it was to be given to her uncle. I should like to add one more beatitude* to those of the gospels and to say, Blessed are they who heal us of self-despisings. Of all services which can be done to man, I know of none more precious.

When I went back to my work I worshipped Theresa, and was entirely overcome with unhesitating absorbing love for her. I saw nothing more of her that day nor the next day. Her uncle told me that she had gone into the country, and that probably she would not return for some time, as she had purposed paying a lengthened visit to a friend at a distance. I had a mind to write to her; but I felt as I have often felt before in great crises, a restraint which was gentle and incomprehensible, but nevertheless unmistakable. I suppose it is not what would be called conscience, as conscience is supposed to decide solely between right and wrong, but it was none the less peremptory, although its voice was so soft and low that it might easily have been overlooked. Over and over again, when I have purposed doing a thing, have I been impeded or arrested by this same silent monitor, and never have I known its warnings to be the mere false alarms of fancy.

After a time, the thought of Mary recurred to

me. I was distressed to find that, in the very height of my love for Theresa, my love for Mary continued unabated. Had it been otherwise, had my affection for Mary grown dim, I should not have been so much perplexed, but it did not. It may be ignominious to confess it, but so it was; I simply record the fact. I had not seen Mardon since that last memorable evening at his house, but one day, as I was sitting in the shop, who should walk in but Mary herself. The meeting, although strange, was easily explained. Her father was ill, and could do nothing but read. Wollaston published freethinking books, and Mardon had noticed in an advertisement the name of a book which he particularly wished to see. Accordingly he sent Mary for it. She pressed me very much to call on him. He had talked about me a good deal, and had written to me at the last address he knew, but the letter had been returned through the dead letter office. It was a week before I could go, and when I did go, I found him much worse than I had imagined him to be. There was no virulent disease of any particular organ, but he was slowly wasting away from atrophy, and he knew, or thought he knew, he should not recover. But he was perfectly self-possessed. 'With regard to immortality,' he said, 'I never know what men mean by it. *What* self is it which is to be immortal? Is it really desired by anybody that he should continue to exist for ever with his

present limitations and failings? Yet if these are not
continued, the man does not continue, but something else, a totally different person. I believe in
the survival of life and thought. People think
that is not enough. They say they want the survival of their personality. It is very difficult to
express any conjecture upon the matter, especially
now when I am weak, and I have no system—
nothing but surmises. One thing I am sure of,
that a man ought to rid himself as much as possible of the miserable egotism which is so anxious
about self, and should be more and more anxious
about the Universal.' Mardon grew slowly worse.
The winter was coming on, and as the tempera-
ture fell, and the days grew darker, he declined.
With all his heroism and hardness he had a weakness or two, and one was, that he did not want to
die in London or be buried there. So we got him
down to Sandgate near Hythe, and procured lodging for him close to the sea, so that he could lie
in bed and watch the sun and moon rise over the
water. Mary, of course, remained with him, and
I returned to London. Towards the end of November I got a letter, to tell me that if I wished to see
him alive again, I must go down at once. I went
that day, and I found that the doctor had been,
and had said that before the morning the end
must come. Mardon was perfectly conscious, in
no pain, and quite calm. He was just able to
speak. When I went into his bedroom, he smiled,

and without any preface or introduction he said: 'Learn not to be over-anxious about meeting troubles and solving difficulties which time will meet and solve for you.' Excepting to ask for water, I don't think he spoke again. All that night Mary and I watched in that topmost garret looking out over the ocean. It was a night entirely unclouded, and the moon was at the full. Towards daybreak her father moaned a little, then became quite quiet, and just as the dawn was changing to sunrise, he passed away. What a sunrise it was! For about half-an-hour before the sun actually appeared, the perfectly smooth water was one mass of gently heaving opaline lustre. Not a sound was to be heard, and over in the south-east hung the planet Venus. Death was in the chamber, but the surpassing splendour of the pageant outside arrested us, and we sat awed and silent. Not till the first burning point of the great orb itself emerged above the horizon, not till the day awoke with its brightness and brought with it the sounds of the day and its cares, did we give way to our grief. It was impossible for me to stay. It was not that I was obliged to get back to my work in London, but I felt that Mary would far rather be alone, and that it would not be proper for me to remain. The woman of the house, in which the lodgings were, was very kind, and promised to do all that was necessary. It was arranged that I should come down again to the funeral. So I went

back to London. Before I had got twenty miles
on my journey the glory of a few hours before had
turned into autumn storm. The rain came down
in torrents, and the wind rushed across the country in great blasts, stripping the trees, and driving
over the sky with hurricane speed great masses
of continuous cloud, which mingled earth and
heaven. I thought of all the ships which were
on the sea in the night, sailing under the serene
stars which I had seen rise and set; I thought
of Mardon lying dead, and I thought of Mary.
The simultaneous passage through great emotions
welds souls, and begets the strongest of all forms
of love. Those who have sobbed together over a
dead friend, who have held one another's hands
in that dread hour, feel a bond of sympathy, pure
and sacred, which nothing can dissolve. I went
to the funeral as appointed. There was some little
difficulty about it, for Mary, who knew her father
so well, was unconquerably reluctant that an in-
consistency should crown the career of one who,
all through life, had been so completely self-accor-
dant. She could not bear that he should be buried
with a ceremony which he despised, and she was
altogether free from that weakness which induces
a compliance with the rites of the Church from
persons who avow themselves sceptics. At last a
burying-ground was found, belonging to a little
half-forsaken Unitarian chapel; and there Mardon was laid. A few friends came from London,

one of whom had been a Unitarian minister, and he 'conducted the service,' such as it was. It was of the simplest kind. The body was taken to the side of the grave, and before it was lowered a few words were said, calling to mind all the virtues of him whom we had lost. These the speaker presented to us with much power and sympathy. He did not merely catalogue a disconnected string of excellences, but he seemed to plant himself in the central point of Mardon's nature, and to see from what it radiated. He then passed on to say that about immortality, as usually understood, he knew nothing; but that Mardon would live as every force in nature lives—for ever; transmuted into a thousand different forms; the original form utterly forgotten, but never perishing. The cloud breaks up and comes down upon the earth in showers which cease, but the clouds and the showers are really undying. This may be true, but, after all, I can only accept the fact of death in silence, as we accept the loss of youth and all other calamities. We are able to see that the arrangements which we should make, if we had the control of the universe, would be more absurd than those which prevail now. We are able to see that an eternity of life in one particular form, with one particular set of relationships, would be misery to many and mischievous to everybody; however sweet those relationships may be to some of us. At times we are reconciled to death as the great

regenerator, and we pine for escape from the sur-
roundings of which we have grown weary; but
we can say no more, and the hour of illumination
has not yet come. Whether it ever will come to a
more nobly developed race, we cannot tell.

Thus far*goes the manuscript which I have in
my possession. I know that there is more of it,
but all my search for it has been in vain. Possibly
some day I may be able to recover it. My friend
discontinued his notes for some years, and consequently the concluding portion of them was entirely separate from the earlier portion, and this
is the reason, I suppose, why it is missing. Miss
Mardon soon followed her father. She caught cold
at his funeral; the seeds of consumption developed
themselves with remarkable rapidity, and in less
than a month she had gone. Her father's peculiar
habits had greatly isolated him, and Miss Mardon
had scarcely any friends. Rutherford went to see
her continually, and during the last few nights
sat up with her, incurring not a little scandal and
gossip, to which he was entirely insensible. For
a time he was utterly broken-hearted; and not
only broken-hearted, but broken-spirited, and incapable of attacking the least difficulty. All the
springs of his nature were softened, so that if anything was cast upon him, there it remained without hope, and without any effort being made to
remove it. He only began to recover when he was

forced to give up work altogether and take a long holiday. To do this he was obliged to leave Mr. Wollaston, and the means of obtaining his much-needed rest were afforded him, partly by what he had saved, and partly by the kindness of one or two whom he had known. I thought that Miss Mardon's death would permanently increase my friend's intellectual despondency, but it did not. On the contrary, he gradually grew out of it. A crisis seemed to take a turn just then, and he became less involved in his old speculations, and more devoted to other pursuits. I fancy that something happened; there was some word revealed to him, or there was some recoil, some healthy horror of eclipse in this self-created gloom which drove him out of it. He accidentally renewed his acquaintance with the butterfly catcher, who was obliged to leave the country and come up to London. He, however, did not give up his old hobby, and the two friends used every Sunday in summer time to sally forth some distance from town and spend the whole live-long day upon the downs and in the green lanes of Surrey. Both of them had to work hard during the week. Rutherford, who had learned shorthand when he was young, got employment upon a newspaper, and ultimately a seat in the gallery of the House of Commons. He never took to collecting insects like his companion, nor indeed to any scientific pursuits, but he certainly changed. I find it very difficult to describe exactly what the change was, because it was into nothing positive; into no sect, party, nor special mode. He did not, for example, go off into absolute denial. I remember his telling me, that to suppress speculation would be a violence done to our nature as unnatural as if we were to prohibit ourselves from looking up to the blue depths between the stars at night; as if we were to determine that nature required correcting in this respect, and that we ought to be so constructed as not to be able to see anything but the earth and what lies on it. Still, these things in a measure ceased to worry him, and the long conflict died away gradually into a peace not formally concluded, and with no specific stipulations, but nevertheless definite. He was content to rest and wait. Better health and time, which does so much for us, brought this about. The passage of years gradually relaxed his anxiety about death by loosening his anxiety for life without loosening his love of life. But I would rather not go into any further details, because I still cherish the hope that some day or the other I may recover the contents of the diary. I am afraid that up to this point he has misrepresented himself, and that those who read his story will think him nothing but a mere egoist, selfish and self-absorbed. Morbid he may have been, but selfish he was not. A more perfect friend I never knew, nor one more capable of complete abandonment to a person for whom he had any real regard, and I can only hope that it may be my good fortune to find the materials which will enable me to represent him autobiographically in a somewhat different light to that in which he appears now.

Notes on the Book of Job
Principles
A Mysterious Portrait

NOTES ON THE BOOK OF JOB

HERE is a book which has for its subject not this or that remote question which touches us only in idle or careless moods: it is a book which deals directly with one of the deepest problems which have occupied the mind of man.

We are a long way towards understanding anything under our consideration when we have properly laid it open, even without comment. Job is a wealthy and blameless man in whom God takes pride, and when Satan presents himself before God, God asks him whether he has considered Job. God thinks Job something worth consideration. Satan stands for the sceptic. He sneers at Job's virtue. Job is well paid for his piety. It is easy for a pious man to be good, but if his prosperity departs he will curse; his creed is the product of his circumstances. God, who is Job's Maker, is, on the other hand, a believer. He stands by Job, puts a stake on him, and authorises Satan to try him. Job loses all his children and his property, and he knows not what is intended by the loss. He is ignorant of what has passed between God and Satan; the secret transactions of the high heavens are unrevealed to him, but nevertheless he is steadfast. What he loses was not his, and in the depths of his sorrow he blesses the name of the Lord. Satan again presents himself before God, and God justly claims the victory —'he holdeth fast his integrity.' Satan replies that Job as yet has not known the worst, and that sickness is the test of all tests. With health a man may endure

anything, but if that fail, it will be seen what becomes
of his religion. God is still confident, and Job is smitten
with sore boils from head to foot. The torment cannot
be surpassed, for not only is it extreme taken by itself,
but it is aggravated by the contrast with his former condition. Death of course presents itself to him as the
welcome end, and he thinks of suicide, suggested to him
by his wife. If he could have but a word of explanation
he could bear all with patience. But no word comes;
the sky gives no sign. Separation from those he has
loved, loathsome disease infecting him up to his very
brain, are terrible, but the real agony is the silence, the
ignorance of the why and the wherefore, the sphinx-like*
imperturbability which meets his prayers. Nevertheless
he sins not. 'What! we have received good at the hand
of God, and shall we not receive evil?' God had been
gracious to him; he recollects all the benefits bestowed
on him, and he refuses to turn upon Him because of
present reverses. He submits; he is unable to explain,
but still he submits.

His three friends forsake him not, but visit him. When
they see him afar off they rend their mantles, sprinkle
dust upon their heads, and coming near to him, say
nothing for seven days and seven nights, for they see that
his grief is very great. The consolation offered by these
three men to Job has passed into a proverb; but who
that knows what most modern consolation is can prevent
a prayer that Job's comforters may be his? They do not
call upon him for an hour, and invent excuses for the
departure which they so anxiously await; they do not
write notes to him and go about their business as if

nothing had happened; they do not inflict on him meaningless commonplaces. They honour him by remaining with him, and by their mute homage, and when they speak to him, although they are mistaken, they offer him the best that they have been able to think. Eliphaz the Temanite, Bildad the Shuhite, and Zophar the Naamathite, sitting in the dust with Job, not daring to intrude upon him, are for ever an example of what man once was and ought to be to man.

After a while, Job 'opened his mouth and cursed his day,' in words which are so vital that they are an everlasting formula for all those of the sons of men whose only hope is their last sleep. There the wicked cease from troubling, and there the weary be at rest.* There the prisoners rest together; they hear not the voice of the oppressor. The small and great are there, and the servant is free from his master. One touch, that in the twenty-fifth verse of the third chapter, is so intense, that it must be the record of a very vivid experience. 'For the thing which I greatly feared is come upon me, and that which I was afraid of is come unto me,' or more correctly, 'For I fear a fear; it meets me; and what I shudder at comes to me.' The object of the dread which haunts us does not generally become real to us, but to Job the horror of all his worst dreams had become actual.

Job's three friends begin their reply, and Eliphaz is the first. He asserts generally the just rule of God, and the connection between doing good and prosperity on the one hand, and between evil-doing and adversity on the other, ending with an amplification of the text that the man is happy whom God correcteth, for by chastisement are we redeemed. Nothing that Eliphaz says is commonplace, although it has no direct bearing on Job's case. If he had been a fool he would never have been dear to Job, nor would he have been one of the three amongst all Job's acquaintances who came to him from afar. We must remember, too, that in a simple, honest society righteousness and temporal prosperity, sin and poverty, may be more immediately conjoined than they are with ourselves, and that Eliphaz may have felt that much that he said was true, although to us it is mere talk. Eliphaz is partly a rhetorician, and, like all persons with that gift, he is frequently carried off his feet and ceases to touch the firm earth. His famous vision in the night, which caused the hair of his flesh to stand up, is an exaggeration, and does nothing but declare what might as well have been declared without it, that man is not just in the eyes of perfect purity. On the other hand, his eloquence assists him to golden sayings which will never be forgotten. Such, for example, are the verses: 'Thou shalt be hid from the scourge of the tongue; neither shalt thou be afraid of destruction when it cometh. At destruction and famine thou shalt laugh; neither shalt thou be afraid of the beast of the earth. For thou shalt be in league with the stones of the field, and the beasts of the field shall be at peace with thee.' The main moments of the oration of Eliphaz are these. Rest upon thy piety; no one who is innocent has perished. In the eyes of God the purest is impure; His angels He charges with folly. The fool may take root, but suddenly his habitation is cursed. Commit your cause unto God who doeth great things and unsearchable, and think yourself happy in His correction. Doing this He will deliver you; you shall come to a good old age and die in peace.

It will be seen that there is here no direct imputation of crime against Job. Eliphaz holds generally nevertheless to the belief that crime is followed by punishment. A certain want of connection and pertinence is observable in him. A man who is made up of what he hears or reads always lacks unity and directness. Confronted by any difficulty or by any event which calls upon him, he answers, not by any operation of his intellect on what is immediately before him, but by detached remarks which he has collected, and which are never a fused homogeneous whole. In conversation he is the same, and will first propound one irrelevant principle and then another—the one, however, not leading to the other, and sometimes contradicting it. The transition from Eliphaz to Job in this respect is very remarkable. The sixth and seventh chapters are molten from end to end, and run in one burning stream. He complains that Eliphaz is beside the mark. 'How forcible are right words! but what doth your arguing reprove?' Eliphaz is like the torrent which the caravans expected, but, when they came to it, it had been consumed out of its place, and they were ashamed. Barren sand was all that was offered instead of the living water. Everything which can be said by a sick man against life is in these chapters. The whole of a vast subsequent literature is summed up here, and he who has once read it may fairly ask never to be troubled with anything more on that side. Death to Job is as the shadow for which he looks as an hireling looks for the reward of his work. He calls upon God to remember that his life is wind; that as a cloud is consumed and vanisheth away, so he that goeth down to the grave shall come up no more; and therefore he prays for consideration. What is man, too, that the Almighty should set Himself against him? 'Supposing I have sinned, what can I do unto Thee? Why set me up as a mark against Thee? Why dost Thou not pardon my transgression?' There is nothing in all poetry more sublime than this: it was a complete answer to Eliphaz, and is a complete answer to all those who suppose that God, after the fashion of a man, proposes to punish man deliberately for his trivial misdeeds, and to punish him, too, not that he may be cured, but because the dignity of the Maker has received an affront.

Bildad, unaffected by what he has heard, referring to it in no way whatever, reiterates the old tale. It is the testimony of the fathers. We are but of yesterday, and know nothing. Age after age has declared that although the wicked may be green before the sun, and his branch shoot forth in his garden, he will be destroyed, and God will not cast away a perfect man.* The confidence of Bildad and his friends upon this point is very remarkable. It must have been based upon something. Such a creed did not grow up without some root; and it is equally curious if it was the result of a philosophy, a felt impossibility to consider God as unjust, or if it was an induction from observed facts. If it was due to a philosophy, it at least bears testimony to the authority of the *ought* in the minds of these men and the depth of the distinction between justice and injustice; injustice being so hateful to them, that in spite of everything which seems to prove the contrary, they were unable to ascribe it to God. If it was an induction from the facts—an induction which, as I have before observed, might in those times be perfectly valid—then it is no less remarkable that such a theocracy should ever have existed.

Job makes no direct answer. 'How shall I contend with Him? I cannot answer one of his thousand questions!' The conception of God in Job's mind has greatly enlarged, and he dwells upon his incomprehensibility. He is the maker of Arcturus, Orion, and the Pleiades,* of that which is farthest from us. 'He goeth by me, and I see Him not; He passeth on also, but I perceive Him not.' He is for ever before me and about me; what He does I see perpetually, but I know Him not. How can I plead with such a being? 'If I had called, and He had answered me, yet I would not believe that He had hearkened unto my voice.' One thing Job knows. 'He destroyeth the perfect and the wicked . . . the earth is given into the hand of the wicked; He covereth the faces of the judges thereof; if not, who is it?' What is the use of debating with Him? 'For He is not a man, as I am, that I should answer Him, and we should come together in judgment. Neither is there any daysman betwixt us that might lay his hand upon us both,' or as the Vulgate* says, '*Non est qui utrumque valeat arguere, et ponere manum suam in ambobus*'—a saying which has in it a grandeur as of some mountain summit 'holding dark communion with the cloud.' Nevertheless can God carelessly cast aside the works of His hands?—so much care apparently has been bestowed upon it. 'Hast Thou not poured me

out as milk, and curdled me like cheese? Thou hast
clothed me with skin and flesh, and hast fenced me with
bones and sinews. Thou hast granted me life and flavour,
and Thy visitation hath preserved my spirit. And these
things hast Thou hid in Thy heart: I know that this is
with Thee,' *i.e.*, was intended by Thee. This book in a
sense is terribly modern, for this is a question which is
continually but resultlessly asked by us all. A woman
of seven-and-twenty died the other day. She was German, and had been in England five or six years. She
had applied herself with such diligence to learning
English, that she spoke it without the least perceptible
accent. She knew French just as well, and her general
training, the result of years of most strenuous work, was
most accurate. She was handsome, and had been married to an English husband two years. One child was
born, and her friends rejoiced at the chances it would
have with a German mother in England. It was a pre-
ternaturally bright child, and it was destroyed—a year
old. Three months before its death the mother began
to show signs of consumption, and now she has gone.
As I stood by her grave, the thought came into my mind
—His hands had made and fashioned her: why then did
He kill her? Why was all this carefully, drop-by-drop
collected store, precious beyond calculation, emptied
on the ground? I know not. I cannot answer him one
of a thousand!

The example of Job protects us from the charge of
blasphemy in not suppressing our doubts. Nothing can
be more daring than his interrogations. There is no
impiety whatever in them, nor are they recognised as

impious in the final chapters of the book. The question is put to us directly by him—it is no creation of ours—and shall we be thought irreverent because we hear it?

Zophar now ventures to express in plain words what before had been merely a hint. 'God exacteth of thee less,' says he, 'than thy iniquity deserveth.' What was observed to be true of Eliphaz is true of Zophar. He is made up of disjointed propositions accumulated from time to time, and now inappropriately vented on Job. For example: 'Thou hast said, my doctrine is pure, and I am clean in Thine eyes. But oh that God would speak, and open His lips against thee; and that He would show thee the secrets of wisdom, that they are double to that which is (double thine own—*et quod multiplex esset lex ejus*: Vulg.); know therefore that God exacteth of thee less than thine iniquity deserveth. Canst thou by searching find out God? canst thou find out the Almighty unto perfection? It is high as heaven; what canst thou do? deeper than hell; what canst thou know?' All this about the incomprehensibility of God is true and great, but what has it to do with the preceding assertion of Job's sin? It is something gathered, something Zophar had been told, and something he has had the wit to feel and admire, but it is not Zophar himself.

Job holds fast to the evidence of his own eyes. 'I have understanding as well as you; I am not inferior to you.' Zophar had appealed to antiquity. Job appeals to the beasts, 'and they shall teach thee; and the fowls of the air, and they shall tell thee.' Of all that happens God is the cause. 'With Him is strength and wisdom: the deceived and the deceiver are His.' It is curious to see what the image of this book becomes after it has passed through the refracting glass of orthodoxy. In the heading to the twelfth chapter we are told, as a summary of the seventh and following verses, that Job *acknowledgeth the general doctrine of God's omnipotency*, and so the texts, 'the deceived and the deceiver are His,' 'He removeth away the speech of the trusty' (*i.e.* of the confident), 'and taketh away the understanding of the aged. He taketh away the heart of the chief of the people of the earth, and causeth them to wander in a wilderness where there is no way. They grope in the dark without light, and He maketh them to stagger like a drunken man'— words tremendous and dangerous—are smothered up under the decent formula of *the general doctrine of God's omnipotency*. It is in fact a very particular doctrine, and not by any means the harmless platitude of the theologians. The difference is great between the preacher in gown and bands acknowledging the general doctrine of God's omnipotency, and Job, who is forced to break away from the faith of his church, sacred through the testimony of ages of miracle and prophecy—Job, who feels the ground shake under him as he is compelled to admit that He whom he worshipped holds both cheat and victim in His hand, smites the eloquent with paralytic stammerings, turns the old man into a melancholy childish driveller, and causes nations to swerve aside over precipices, under the guidance of leaders whom He has blinded. Job is the type of those great thinkers who cannot compromise; who cannot say *but yet;* who faithfully follow their intellect to its very last results, and admit all its conclusions. They are better to a man so constituted than living in a fool's paradise, however paradisiacal it may be. 'For,' translating the twelfth verse of the thirteenth chapter into intelligibility by the help of the German Version, 'your sayings are sayings of ashes; your ramparts are ramparts of mud'—mere mud before the attack thinks Job, although the fool may dwell behind them in placid content, believing them to be granite.

Job renews his desire to speak with God. He renews also his request for death; and yet death, the passing of life like a shadow, is to him most pathetic, although the pathos in his case had never been sharpened by the loss of a hope in immortality. 'His sons came to honour, and he knoweth it not; and they are brought low, but he perceiveth it not of them. But *his* flesh upon him shall have pain, and *his* soul within him shall mourn.' He is shut out from all sympathy with the joys and the sorrows of the children whom he has so much loved. He lies cold and dead, when they are exulting in love, in marriage, in well-deserved gratulations from their fellows. He is cold and dead, when they are in complicated difficulty or distress from which he could save them!

The three friends, having each said what they had to say, and Job having answered, begin again, Eliphaz taking the lead as before. His position is unaltered. How should it be altered? It is not possible for a man committed, as Eliphaz and his companions are committed, to alter, whatever the facts may be, and the same argument returns with little variation. Eliphaz condemns Job because his talk can do no good. Always has this been urged against those who, with no thought of consequences, cannot but utter that which is in them; and it is held to be especially pertinent against the man who, like Job, challenges the constitution under which he lives, and 'has no remedy to propose.' It is incredible to Eliphaz that there should be anything in Job's case which had not been anticipated. 'Art thou the first man that was born? Hast thou heard the secret of God?' This was supposed to be conclusive in Job's day, and has been thought to be conclusive ever since.

Although there must necessarily be a certain monotony in the continuous counter-statements of Job, there is not a single dead repetition. For example, in this second answer to Eliphaz, Job, after the retort that he, too, 'could heap up words' if he pleased, adds, 'my purposes are broken off, even the thoughts of my heart.' Happy is the man, no matter what his lot may be otherwise, who sees some tolerable realisation of the design he has set before him in his youth or in his earlier manhood. Many there are who, through no fault of theirs, know nothing but mischance and defeat. Either sudden calamity overturns in tumbling ruins all that they had painfully toiled to build, and success for ever afterwards is irrecoverable; or, what is most frequent, each day brings its own special hindrance, in the shape of ill-health, failure of power, or poverty, and a fatal net is woven over the limbs preventing all activity. The youth with his dreams wakes up some morning, and finds himself fifty years old with not one solitary achievement, with nothing properly learned, with nothing properly done, with an existence consumed in mean, miserable, squalid cares, and his goal henceforth is the grave in which to hide himself ashamed.

Bildad's second response travels over the old ground. 'The light of the wicked shall be put out, and the spark of his fire shall not shine,' &c., &c., and Job reiterates that all this is nothing but clatter. 'Know now that God hath overthrown me, and hath compassed me with His net. Behold, I cry out of wrong, but I am not heard: I cry aloud, but there is no judgment. He hath fenced up my way that I cannot pass, and He hath set darkness in my paths.' Into the much disputed question of the meaning of the famous verses at the end of the 19th chapter, which have been so generally supposed to refer to the resurrection, I cannot enter. I do not know what they mean, and it is a pity that commentators, where there is no certain light, cannot say there is none, but feel themselves compelled to give an interpretation. I will only go so far as to admit that if there be any allusion to future life here, much of what goes before and comes after is obscured. We are at a loss to know why Job should have dwelt upon the finality of death if he had immortality before him. It is inconsistent with the thought that he was about to go 'whence he should not return,' and it destroys the parallel between the flower, which revives at the scent of water, and man who 'giveth up the ghost, and where is he?'—man who 'lieth down and riseth not: till the heavens be no more they shall not awake nor be raised out of their sleep.' It is curious, too, that Job's friends do not allude to the doctrine, as one would think they would certainly do, at least after having seen Job's reliance upon it. Zophar's speech in

the 20th chapter does not refer to it. He contents himself
with the affirmation that in *this* life the avenger of the
wicked will appear: 'The increase of his house shall
depart—shall flow away in the day of his wrath. *This*
is the portion of a wicked man from God, and the heritage appointed unto him by God."

As the action of the poem proceeds, Job becomes more
and more direct. 'Mark me,' says he in the 21st chapter,
'and be astonished, and lay your hand upon your mouth.
Even when I reflect I am afraid, and trembling taketh
hold on my flesh. Wherefore do the wicked live, become
old, yea, are mighty in power?' They openly defy God.
They say, 'What is the Almighty that we should serve
Him?' and yet 'their bull gendereth, and faileth not,
their cow calveth, and slippeth not her calf.' His friends,
in order to avoid the significance of what is obvious, had
explained it away by the assumption that iniquity is
laid up for the children of the wicked. 'His own eyes,'
replies Job, 'ought to see his destruction, and he himself
ought to drink of the wrath of the Almighty. For what
care hath he in his house after him, when the number
of his months is cut off in the midst?' Good and evil
'lie down alike in the dust, and the worms do cover
them.' The closing verses of the chapter must be given
as they stand: 'Behold, I know your thoughts, and the
devices that ye wrongfully imagine against me. For ye
say, where is the house of the prince? and where the
tent of the dwellings of the wicked? Have ye not asked
them that go by the way, and do ye not know their
tokens (*i.e.*, do ye not know what travellers will tell
you), that the wicked is spared at the day of destruc-

tion: they are led away at the day of wrath? who shall
declare his way to his face? and who shall repay him
what he hath done? He is brought to the grave, and over
his tomb is watch kept. The clods of the valley are
sweet unto him, and every man draws after him, and
innumerable before him. How, then, comfort ye me in
vain! Your answers are but falsehood.' Once more
Job takes his stand on actual eyesight. He relies, too,
on the testimony of those who have travelled. He prays
his friends to turn away from tradition, from the idle and
dead ecclesiastical reiteration of what had long since
ceased to be true, and to look abroad over the world,
to hear what those have to say who have been outside
the narrow valleys of Uz.* Job demands of his opponents
that they should come out into the open universe. If
they will but lift up their eyes across the horizon which
hitherto has hemmed them in, what enlargement will
not thereby be given to them! Herein lies the whole
contention of the philosophers against the preachers.
The philosophers ask nothing more than that the conception of God should be wide enough to cover *what we
see*: that it should not be arbitrarily framed to serve
certain ends; that it shall be inclusive of everything
which is discovered beyond Uz and its tabernacles; and
if the conclusions we desire cannot be drawn from that
conception, so much the worse for them.

Inexpressibly touching is the last verse but one. It is
a revelation of the inmost heart striving to be at peace
with death. Not one grain of comfort is sought outside,
and it is this which makes it so precious. There is not
even a hint of a hope. All is drawn from within, and is

solid and real. To this we can come when religion, dreams, metaphysics, all fail. The clods of the valley shall be sweet even to us. Why should we complain, why should we be in mortal fear! We do but go the path which the poorest, the weakest, the most timid have all trodden; which the poorest, the weakest, the most timid for millions of years will still tread. Every man draws after us, and innumerable have drawn thither before us. None who have passed have ever rebelled or repented, nor shall we. Job, in building on rest, and on community, has struck the adamant which cannot be shaken.

So strong is the superstition of the friends that Eliphaz now advances to a creation of crimes which Job *must* have committed. It is more easy to believe him to be a sinner than that their creed can be shaken. 'Thou hast taken,' says Eliphaz, 'a pledge from thy brother for nought, and stripped the naked of their clothing. Thou hast not given water to the weary to drink, and thou hast withholden bread from the hungry. But as for the mighty man, he had the earth; and the honourable man dwelt in it. Thou hast sent widows away empty, and the arms of the fatherless have been broken. There-fore snares are round about thee, and sudden fear troubleth thee.' There was no shadow of truth in the accusation. Job seems, on the contrary, to have been remarkable for the virtues which were the very opposite of these sins. It is worth while to notice how our meas-ure of wrong has altered. To Eliphaz, wrong, when he wishes specially to name it, is a class of actions, not one of which is to us accounted an offence, except by certain

sentimental persons. A man now-a-days may be a good
Christian and a good citizen, and do every one of these
deeds which in Job's time were so peculiarly reprehen-
sible, and which are taken, as we shall see afterwards,
with Job's full consent, as the very type of misdoing.
Eliphaz, as before observed, is the church. But what a
world that must have been, when the church's anathe-
mas were reserved for him who exacted pledges from
his brother, who neglected the famishing, and who paid
undue respect to the great. Job's answer is an indignant
denial of the charge. It is not worth an answer, and
again he implores God to speak to him. 'Behold, I go
forward, but He is not there; and backward, but I cannot perceive Him; on the right hand where He doth
work, but I cannot behold Him: He hideth Himself on
the right hand, that I cannot see Him.' Job adds to the
last repetition, however, of his complaint something
which is new—that He is irreversible. He is 'in one
mind:' more probably the Unexampled, the Unique—
'and who can turn Him?' and he proceeds in the next
verse to a still plainer exposition. 'He performeth the
thing that is appointed for me: and many such things
are with Him. Therefore I am troubled at His presence:
when I consider I am afraid of Him. For God maketh
my heart soft, and the Almighty troubleth me.' The
temptation is great, when we find anything approaching
modern learning in an ancient book, to suppose that we
have got hold of an anticipation of it, but we cannot
conclude from this passage that Job's belief in the impossibility of altering the divine decree is our belief in
the uniformity of nature. Nevertheless Job's dejection,

because no man can turn Him, and the fear at His presence, because He performeth the thing appointed, are the dejection and the fear of our nineteenth century as certainly as they were those of the seventh century B.C.

In the twenty-fourth chapter Job turns aside from the charge brought by Zophar against him, and points to what cannot be disputed, the success of the wandering savage tribes, which must have made such a figure in the domestic history of the time. They, says Job, go on their desperate way unrebuked, and die as the others die. 'Drought and heat consume the snow waters; so doth the grave those which have sinned.' These are they who 'are wet with the showers of the mountains, and embrace the rock for want of a shelter.'

The controversy has now been fully developed. Bildad mumbles in half-a-dozen weak words, what is nothing to the point, that man in God's sight must be unclean. His short monologue sounds rather as a meditation meant for himself, the only refuge he could find from the difficulty which pressed upon him. Zophar, who ought to have spoken again, is silent. The victory remains with Job, and he sums up his case.

First of all, he competes as it were with Bildad in his account of the Almighty. It is as if Job said—I also know Him and what He is. 'Hast thou plentifully declared the thing as it is?' and then he describes God as hanging the earth upon nothing, as the Maker of the constellations, and yet these are but the very fringe of His doings; 'what a mere whisper of Him do we hear; but the thunder of His power who shall understand?' He holds fast too, by his integrity. Nothing that his

friends have urged will convince him against his own
clear conscience. He remains to them in an utterly un-
converted and even horribly profane state of mind—
'My heart is not ashamed for one of my days.' He casts
up his accounts, and refuses to allow any sin, actual or
imputed, open or secret. The rest of the 27th chapter
is a mystery which is insoluble. It stands in Job's name,
but it is an admission of everything which he had before
denied. 'This is the portion of a wicked man with God,
and the heritage of oppressors, which they shall receive
of the Almighty. If his children be multiplied, it is for
the sword; and his offspring shall not be satisfied with
bread.' In the 21st chapter Job had urged on this very
point, 'Let his *own* eyes' the eyes of the wrong-doer himself—'see his destruction.' Again in the 21st chapter,
'Their seed is established in their sight with them, and
their offspring before their eyes.' In the 27th chapter
'terrors take hold on him as waters, a tempest stealeth
him away in the night.' In the 21st chapter 'their houses
are safe from fear . . . they spend their days in wealth,
and in a moment go down to the grave. Therefore they
say unto God, Depart from us.' Whether in the 27th
chapter there is a remnant of a speech by Zophar, from
whom one is due, or whether it is an interpolation de-
vised to save Job's orthodoxy, I have no means of deter-
mining, but that it is unintelligible is certain, and the
only thing to be done with it is to pass it by. The 28th
chapter is not free from difficulty, and both the 27th and
28th are rendered doubly suspicious by the commence-
ment of the 29th. 'Moreover, Job continued his parable
and said,' the sequel being a reversion to the old pang

so authentic and so familiar: 'Oh that I were as in months past.' But the 28th chapter is so exquisite, that even if it does not help the development of the poem, or is inharmonious with it, it cannot be neglected. It is a passionate personification of Wisdom, and the desire for her is almost sensuous in its intensity. 'It cannot be gotten for gold, neither shall silver be weighed for the price thereof. It cannot be valued with the gold of Ophir,* with the precious onyx, or the sapphire.' This is the wisdom by which the world was framed; by which the winds and waters were measured 'when He made a decree for the rain, and a way for the lightning of the thunder.' This very same wisdom it is which is the fear of the Lord. 'Unto man he said, Behold, the fear of the Lord, that is wisdom; and to depart from evil is understanding.' It is wisdom in both cases—the same wisdom. It is not going beyond the text to say that this is what it teaches. What we call morality is no separate science. It is the science by which a decree was made for the rain and a way for the lightning of the thunder. These immortal words should not be narrowed down to the poverty-stricken conclusion that the sum-total of all wisdom is conformity to half-a-dozen plain rules, and that the divine ambition of man is to be limited within the bounds of departing from evil. Rather do we discover in these words the essential unity of fearing the Lord and wisdom. To be wise is to fear Him. Wisdom, the wisdom searched out by Him in His creation of the universe, when it is brought down to man, is morality. Whatever we may think of the date of this portion of the book, there is no question as to the three following chapters. Job

protests, not merely his innocence, but his active righteousness, and remembers his past prosperity. He dwells
upon the time when he laughed away his friends' trouble,
and they were not able to darken the cheerfulness of his
countenance. Immovable he was when fear was abroad,
and the hearts of men were shaken. 'I chose out their
way, and sat chief, and dwelt as a king in the army, as
one that comforteth the mourners.' The humanities of
these chapters reveal the best side of the Semitic race.
They are the burden of the prophets—of Micah, who
invokes God's vengeance on those who 'covet fields, and
take them by violence, and houses, and take them away:
so they oppress a man and his house, even a man and
his heritage;'*and they are the soul of the Revolution,
which will one day make foolish the modern quarrels
over forms of government. Job goes down to the very
root of the matter. 'Did not He that made me in the
womb make him? and did not one fashion us in the
womb? If I have withheld the poor from their desire,
or have caused the eyes of the widow to fail; or have
eaten my morsel myself alone, and the fatherless hath
not eaten thereof (for from my youth he was brought
up with me, as with a father, and I have guided her
from my mother's womb); if I have seen any perish for
want of clothing, or any poor without covering; if his
loins have not blessed me, and if he were not warmed
with the fleece of my sheep; if I have lifted up my hand
against the fatherless, when I saw my help in the gate:
then let mine arm fall from my shoulder-blade, and
mine arm be broken from the bone.' Again, let it be
laid to heart that the obligations, the breach of which

was a 'terror' to him, are not one of them legal obligations, and not one of them moral obligations in the
modern sense of the word. The races to whom we owe
the Bible were cruel in war; they were revengeful; their
veins were filled with blood hot with lust; they knew no
art, nor grace, nor dialectic, such as Greece knew, but
one service they at least have rendered to the world.
They have preserved in their prophets and poets this
eternal verity—*He that made me in the womb made him*—
and have proclaimed with divine fury a divine wrath
upon all those who may be seduced into forgetfulness
of it. In discernment of the real breadth and depth of
social duty, nothing has gone beyond the book of Job.
Much of it ought to be engraved upon brass and set
upon pillars throughout the land, as a perpetual reminder of the truth as between man and man. In one
of the shires of this country stands, or used to stand, a
tablet with a mark on it twenty or thirty feet above the
level of the river which runs beneath, and on the tablet
it is recorded, incredible almost to all present inhabitants, that on a certain day years ago the water in a
great flood reached that mark. So with the book of Job.
It is a monument testifying, although its testimony is
now hardly believable, that this was a rich man's notion
of duty; and more extraordinary still, that this was his
religion.

As to Elihu's speech I have nothing to say. Whether
there is sufficient philological evidence*against it I am
unable to determine, but the evidence supplied by the
instinct of the ordinary reader is sufficient. Setting
apart that it is entirely unnecessary in the progress of

the poem, and that it is tame and flat compared with the other portion of it, the omission of Elihu in the prologue and the epilogue is almost decisive.

'Then the Lord answered Job out of the whirlwind.' He makes no reference whatever to what had passed in heaven. It would have been easy, one would think, to have cleared up all Job's doubts by telling him at once that his trials were ordained to establish his steadfastness and confound the Accuser. But no; He does not, and cannot allude to that act of the drama which had been enacted unseen. The very first words of the Almighty are the key to the whole of what follows. 'Where wast thou when I laid the foundations of the earth? declare if thou hast understanding. Who hath laid the measures thereof, if thou knowest? or who hath stretched the line upon it? Whereupon are the foundations thereof fastened? or who laid the corner-stone thereof: when the morning stars sang together, and all the sons of God shouted for joy?' The appeal is in no sense whatever to the bare omnipotence of God. He is omnipotent, but not upon His omnipotence does He rely in His divine argument with Job. Listen, for example, to such passages as these: 'Who hath divided a watercourse for the overflowing of waters, or a way for the lightning of thunder; *to cause it to rain on the earth, where no man is*; on the wilderness, wherein there is no man; to satisfy the desolate and waste ground, and to cause the bud of the tender herb to spring forth?' Still more noteworthy, there is the ostrich, 'which leaveth her eggs in the earth and warmeth them in the dust, and forgetteth that the foot may crush them, or that the wild beast may break them. She is hardened against her young ones as though they were not hers; her labour is in vain without fear; because God hath deprived her of wisdom, neither hath He imparted to her understanding.' There are also the hawk and the eagle: 'Doth the hawk fly by thy wisdom and stretch her wings towards the south? Doth the eagle mount up at thy command, and make his nest on high? He dwelleth and abideth upon the rock, upon the crag of the rock, and the strong place. From thence he seeketh his prey, and his eyes behold afar off. His young ones also suck up blood; and where the slain are, there is he.'

The Almighty pauses. 'Moreover the Lord answered Job and said, 'Shall he who censures God contend with Him? He that reproveth God, let Him answer it.' Job humiliates himself: 'Behold, too insignificant am I; what shall I answer Thee? I will lay mine hand upon my mouth.' Jehovah again speaks from the storm: 'Gird up thy loins now like a man: I will demand of thee, and declare thou unto Me. Wilt thou also disannul My right? wilt thou condemn Me, that thou mayest be righteous? Hast thou an arm like God? or canst thou thunder with a voice like Him? Deck thyself now with majesty and excellency, and array thyself with glory and beauty! Cast abroad the rage of thy wrath: and behold every one that is proud, and abase him! look on every one that is proud, and bring him low, and tread down the wicked in their place! Hide them in the dust together, and bind their faces in secret! Then will I also confess unto thee that thine own right hand can save thee.' The description of behemoth and the leviathan follows.

There are two observations plain enough but most important to be made upon the Divine oration. One is, that God vouchsafes to Job no revelation in order to solve the mystery with which he was oppressed. There is no promise of immortality, nothing but an injunction to open the eyes and look abroad over the universe. Whatever help is to be obtained is to be had, not through an oracle, but by the exercise of Job's own thought.

In the next place, there is no trace of any admission on the part of Jehovah that the well-meant theories of the friends are correct. On the contrary, His wrath is kindled against them. Jehovah does not admit for a moment that He has established any unvarying connection between righteousness and prosperity, sin and adversity.

What then is God's meaning? It behoves us to keep close to the text in our interpretation of it. We have not to ascertain what we might imagine or wish Him to say. We have to find out what He did say. Most scrupulously are we to avoid foisting upon Him any idea of our own. It is much easier to impose a meaning upon the Bible, written in an age so unlike our own, than to extract *the* meaning from it. God reminds us of His wisdom, of the mystery of things, and that man is not the measure of His creation. The world is immense, constructed on no plan or theory which the intellect of man can grasp. It is *transcendent* everywhere. This is the burden of every verse, and is the secret, if there be one, of the poem. Sufficient or insufficient, there is nothing more. Job is to hold fast to the law within; that is his candle which is to light his path: but God is infinite.

Job, if he is not satisfied, submits. Henceforth he will be mute—'once have I spoken, but I will not answer: yea twice; but I will proceed no further.' 'I have uttered that I understood not; things too wonderful for me, which I knew not.' All his thinkings seemed like hearsay. This then was the real God. 'Now mine eye seeth Thee.'

It is impossible to neglect the epilogue in which Job is restored to his prosperity. If we do neglect it, we may perhaps turn the book into something more accordant with our own notions, but the book itself we have not got. There is nothing really inconsistent in it. The Almighty has explained Himself, and the explanation stands, but there is no reason why Job should be left in such utter misery. The anguish which completely envelops the sufferer does break and yield with time, and often disappears. On the other hand, we have no right to demand happiness, and we are not told that Job's happiness returned to him because he demanded it. It is utterly to mistake the purpose of the last chapter to suppose that in it lies the meaning of all that has gone before, and that it teaches us that we have only to wait and God will reward us. God is great, we know not His ways. He takes from us all we have, but yet, if we possess our souls in patience,* we *may* pass the valley of the shadow and come out in sunlight again. We may or we may not. If we had before us a statement of a nineteenth-century philosophy, there would undoubtedly have been no epilogue; but the book is not a philosophy, but a record of an experience.

What more have we to say now than God said from

the whirlwind over 2500 years ago? We have passed through much since that memorable day. We have had new religions which have overspread the world, and yet the sum total of all that we can add is but small. Scientific discovery—astronomy for example—contributes something. The earth is no longer the centre of the starry system, and with the disappearance of that belief much more has disappeared. Man has not become of less importance, but it is seen that all things do not converge to him. We have learned too more intimately God's infinity. It is this which caused Job to put his hand on his mouth—the truth that even the dry clod and the desert grass are dear to Him though no man is near them. Why should they not be? Why should I say that dew falling on a thorn in a desert is wasted, but falling on my flower shows proper economy? Furthermore, if resources are inexhaustible, there can be no waste. It might be waste if *I* were to lavish time and treasure on building up the blue succory perfect in its azure, which springs by the wayside, to be smothered by the chalk dust and to be destroyed in its pride by a chance cut from a boy's stick, but it is no waste to God. In this way the lesson which the whirlwind taught us has been expanded and intensified. We return to it anew after all the creeds, and we say that they are but the hearing of Him, and that this is *seeing* Him.

PRINCIPLES

I HAVE often reproached myself that principles have done so little for me. It is not that I have not got any. I have been for years familiar with all the wisest and noblest principles which are to be found in philosophical and religious books from the time of Moses*downwards. Nor is it a failing of mine that I have not the courage or strength to apply principles. I am weak as other men are, and liable to yield to temptation; but this is not my main difficulty; my trouble is that I never know how to apply my principles. Take a case: It is true that every man ought to be satisfied with the limitations of his own nature. He ought not to repine that he cannot write poems or carve statues. The principle is of some service when the question is of poems or statues; but I should be equally helped without it, for the most uncultivated of mortals is not so foolish as to be melancholy because he cannot fly. At other times, when I most need assistance, and call upon this principle to aid me, I am all adrift. I am placed in such a position, for example, that it is my duty to exercise control over somebody below me. I ought to tell him that he is going wrong and put him right, but I feel that I cannot, and that he is too strong for me. This may be mere conquerable cowardice, or it may be that in this direction I am as limited as I am in relation to poems or statues. I do not know. When I have done what I think I can do, am I to sit down contented and say I can do no more, or am I to listen to a voice which for ever prompts me and whispers, '*All* you can do you have not done'?

During the major portion of my life I am the victim of antagonisms, and each opposing force seems able to plead equal justification. This, however, is the system on which the world is built. It is a mistake to expect a principle to be anything else than abstract. An act is concrete, and that means that it is something in which oppositions find their solution and lie in repose. This, it will be said, leaves us just where we were and gives us no assistance. It is a just criticism. Man is man because he possesses the proud prerogative of actualising the abstract. He is not its fool. In each deed he does he has to be aware of two poles, and say, 'Between them, doing justice to both, I fix this deed *so*.' Instead of two poles there may be a dozen or more, not exactly poles, but divergent or opposite pulls. The richer the nature is, the more there will be of them; the stronger the nature, the more perfect will be the harmony in which they will all meet in external life.

To know principles, although at first it seems as if the consciousness of them is of no service to us, is really an enormous benefit. The more we have, if we have only the gift to manage them, the more real and less shadowy shall we be. Let it ever be remembered that the reality of an act or of a man is in exact proportion to the number of principles which lie in that man or act, and that the single abstract is unreality, unsubstantiality, uselessness. Let us not be cast down at our difficulties. Let us rejoice rather at the exalted, the divine task that is imposed on us. Man is the very top of the creation, the express image of the Creator, because at every moment of his life he resolves abstracts into realities.

The curse of every truth is that a counterfeit of it always waits on it, and is its greatest enemy. What is this which I have said but the mere commonplace that we must never go too far, and that compromise is the rule of life? But between my doctrine and this commonplace there is a great difference. The commonplace teaches that no principle is ultimately efficacious; that it is to be trusted to a certain arbitrary point, and beyond that it somehow ceases to be valid. The truth, on the other hand, is that *every* principle is efficacious up to the uttermost, and that faith in it is never to be abandoned. The compromise comes of imbecility or impotence, and is essentially contrary to the concrete reconciliation of abstracts.

It is difficult to separate morals from wisdom, and in fact no clear line of demarcation is possible; but perhaps we may say that in morals a single clear principle is more distinctly supreme than in wisdom. Morality is the region of the abstract. It is mercifully provided that that which is of the most importance to us in the conduct of life should be under the dominion of the abstract, and therefore be plain to everybody. There is no wit necessary in order to discover what we ought to do when the question is one of telling a lie or speaking the truth. This seems to me as valid a distinction between morality and wisdom as any I know. The abstractness of the moral law gives it a certain sublimity and ideality which is very remarkable.

Perpetual undying faith in principles is of the utmost

importance. I sometimes think it is the very Alpha and
Omega*of life. Belief in principles is the only intelligible
interpretation I have ever been able to attach to the
word faith. A man with faith in principles, even if they
be not first-rate, is sure to succeed. The man who has
no faith in them is sure to fail. Nothing finer after all
can be said of faith than that which is said in the epistle
to the Hebrews, and no finer example can be given
of it than that of Noah there given. Noah was warned
of God that destruction would visit the impious race by
which he was surrounded. He quietly set to work to
build his ark. There is no record that it was built by
miracle, and he must have been a long time about it.
Glorious days of unclouded sunshine with no hint of
rain, weeks perhaps of drought, must have passed over
his head as he sat and wrought at this wondrous structure. Imagine the scoffs of the irreverent Canaanites,*
the jeers of the mob which passed by or peeped over
fences; imagine the suggestions of lunacy! Worse and
worse, imagine what was said and done when, seven
days before the rain, though not a drop had fallen, the
pious man with all his family, and with that wonderful
troop of animals, entered the ark, *and the Lord shut him in.*
But God had spoken to him: he had heard a divine word,
and in that word he believed, despite the absence of a
single fleck of vapour in the sky. What a time, though,
it must have been for him during those seven days!
Would it come true? Would he have to walk out again
down those planks with the clean beasts and unclean
beasts*after him, amidst the inextinguishable laughter
of all his pagan, God-denying neighbours? But in a

week he heard the first growl of the tempest. He was justified, God was justified; and for evermore Noah stands as a divine type of what we call faith. This is really it. What we have once *heard*, really heard in our best moments, by that let us abide. There are multitudes of moments in which intelligent conviction in the truth of principles disappears, and we are able to do nothing more than fall back on mere dogged determinate resolution to go on; not to give up what we have once found to be true. This power of dogged determinate resolution, which acts independently of enthusiasm, is a precious possession. A principle cannot for ever appear to us in its pristine splendour. Not only are we tempted to forsake it by other and counter attractions, but it gets wearisome to us because it is a principle. It becomes a fetter, we think. Then it is that faith comes into operation. We hold fast, and by-and-by a third state follows the second, and we emerge into confidence again. One would like to have a record of all that passed through the soul of Ulysses when he was rowed past the Sirens.* In what intellectually subtle forms did not the desire to stay clothe itself to that intellectually subtle soul? But he had bound himself beforehand, and he reached Ithaca and Penelope* at last. I remember once having determined after much deliberation that I ought to undertake a certain task which would occupy me for years. It was one which I could at any moment relinquish. After six months I began to flag, and my greatest hindrance was, not the confessed desire for rest, but all kinds of the most fascinating principles or pseudo principles, which flattered what was best and not what was

worst in me. I was narrowing my intellect, preventing
the proper enjoyment of life, neglecting the sunshine,
&c. &c. But I thought to myself, 'Now the serpent was
more subtile than any beast of the field,' and that his
temptation specially was that 'your eyes shall be opened,
and ye shall be as gods.' I was enabled to persevere,
oftentimes through no other motive than that aforesaid
divine doggedness, and presently I was rewarded.

As an instance of the necessity of reconciling principles, the experience of advancing years may be taken.
A man must for ever keep himself open to the reception
of new light. As he gets older, he will find that the tendency grows to admit nothing into his mind which does
not corroborate something he has already believed, and
that the new truth acquired is very limited. If he wishes
to keep himself young he must use his utmost efforts to
maintain his susceptibility. He must not converse solely
with himself and turn over and over again the thoughts
of the past. He must not in reading a book dwell upon
those passages only which are a reflection of his own
mind. This is true, but it is also true that he must put
certain principles beyond debate. Life is too short to
admit of the perpetual discussion and re-discussion of
what is fundamental and has been settled after bestow-
ing on it all the care of which we are capable. If, by
reason of patient and long-continued experiment, we
have found out, for example, that a certain regimen is
good for us, we should be foolish, at the bidding of even
a scientific man, to begin experimenting again. We
must simply say that this matter is once for all at rest,
whether rightly or wrongly, and that our days here are

but threescore years and ten. Neither can we afford to make quite certain between opposing principles. The demand for certainty is a sign of weakness, and if we persist in it, induces paralysis. The successful man is he who when he sees that no further certainty is attainable, promptly decides on the most probable side, as if he were completely sure it was right. If we come to a parting of roads, and this one goes slightly east and the other a little west, then, if we believe that our town lies westward, we are bound, supposing we have no other guide, instantaneously to take the western road, although we know that the tracks thereabouts twist in every direction, and that the one to the west may bend southwards and bring us back to the point from which we started.

It is an old theory that our action depends on wisdom. We do what we see to be good. If we really see it to be good, we must do it. There is no doubt that a certain dimness of vision accompanies temptation. We do not discern in its real splendour the virtue which, properly discerned, would fascinate and compel us. But, nevertheless, the part which pure resolution has to play is very great. It is, as Burns says, the stalk of carle hemp* in us. A man must continually put his back to the wall, just as in pain the hero determines through sheer force of will to endure. Inflexibility, Will, the power of holding fast to a principle, is a primary faculty, not altogether to be resolved into insight, although of course it is easy enough to argue the identity of everything in man, and to prove that will is science, or love, or a superior capacity of definition, or anything else. We often fail through a lamentable trick of reopening negotiations with what we have determined to abandon. Severed once and for good reason, let it remain once and for all severed.

Principles are more useful to us in time of danger when they are presented to us incarnated in living men. We should ask ourselves, how would Paul or Jesus have acted in this case. That question will often settle a difficulty when the appeal to abstract principles would only bewilder us through the difficulty of selection. Furthermore, the reference to men rather than to abstractions puts us in good company: we are conscious of society and of fellowship: we see the faces of the heroes looking on us and encouraging us. Plutarch in his essay —*How a man may perceive his own proceeding and going forward in virtue* (Holland's translation)—says, 'Hereupon also it followeth by good consequence that they who have once received so deep an impression in their hearts take this course with themselves, that when they begin any enterprise or enter into the administration of government, or when any sinister accident is presented to them, they set before their eyes the examples of those, who either presently are or heretofore have been worthy persons, discoursing in this manner: What is it that Plato would have done in this case? What would Epaminondas have said to this? How would Lycurgus or Agesilaus*have behaved themselves herein? After this sort (I say) will they labour to frame, compose, reform, and adorn their manners, as it were, before a mirror or looking-glass, to wit, in correcting any unseemly speech that they have let fall, or repressing any passion that hath risen in them. They that have learned the names of the demi-gods called *Idaei Dactyli*know how to use them as counter charms, or preservatives against sudden frights, pronouncing the same one after another readily and ceremoniously; but the remembrance and thinking upon great and worthy men represented suddenly unto those who are in the way of perfection, and taking hold of them in all passions and complexions which shall encounter them, holdeth them up, and keepeth them upright that they cannot fall.' This we know is the secret of the Christian religion. It is based upon a Person, and the whole drift of Paul's epistles is specially this—to turn Christ into a second conscience. More particularly for simple people easily led away, but, indeed, for all people, the importance, the overwhelming importance of maintaining a personal basis for religion, cannot be overstated. I only speak my own experience: I am not talking theology or philosophy. I *know* what I am saying, and can point out the times and places when I should have fallen if I had been able to rely for guidance upon nothing better than a commandment or a deduction. But the pure, calm, heroic image of Jesus confronted me, and I succeeded. I had no doubt as to what *He* would have done, and through Him I did not doubt what I ought to do.

A MYSTERIOUS PORTRAIT

I REMEMBER some years ago that I went to spend a
Christmas with an old friend who was a bachelor.
He might, perhaps, have been verging on sixty at the
time of my visit. On his study wall hung the portrait—
merely the face—of a singularly lovely woman. I did
not like to ask any questions about it. There was no
family likeness to him, and we always thought that early
in life he had been disappointed. But one day, seeing
that I could hardly keep my eyes off it, he said to me,
'I have had that picture for many years, although you
have never seen it before. If you like, I will tell you its
history.' He then told me the following story.

'In the year 1817, I was beginning life, and struggling
to get a living. I had just started in business. I was
alone, without much capital, and my whole energies
were utterly absorbed in my adventure. In those days
the master, instead of employing a commercial traveller,
often used to travel himself, and one evening I had to
start for the North to see some customers. I chose to go
by night in order to save time, and as it was bitterly cold
and I was weakly in the chest, I determined to take a
place inside the coach. We left St. Martin's-le-Grand
at about half-past eight, and I was the sole inside passenger. I could not sleep, but fell into a kind of doze,
which was not sufficiently deep to prevent my rousing
myself at every inn where we changed horses. Nobody
intruded upon me, and I continued in the same drowsy,
half-waking, half-slumbering condition till we came to

the last stage before reaching Eaton Socon.* I was then
thoroughly awake, and continued awake until after the
coach started. But presently I fell sound asleep for,
perhaps, half-an-hour, and woke suddenly. To my great
surprise I found a lady with me. How she came there I
could not conjecture. I was positive that she did not
get in when the coach last stopped. She sat at the opposite corner, so that I could see her well, and a more
exquisite face I thought I had never beheld. It was not
quite English—rather pale, earnest, and abstracted, and
with a certain intentness about the eyes which denoted
a mind accustomed to dwell upon ideal objects. I was
not particularly shy with women, and perhaps if she had
been any ordinary, pretty girl I might have struck up a
conversation with her. But I was dumb, for I hardly
dared to intrude. It would have been necessary to begin
by some commonplaces, and somehow my lips refused
the utterance of commonplaces. Nor was this strange.
If I had happened to find myself opposite the great Lord
Byron in a coach I certainly should not have thrust
myself upon him, and how should I dare to thrust myself
upon a person who seemed as great and grand as he,
although I did not know her name? So I remained
perfectly still, only venturing by the light of the moon
to watch her through my half-shut eyes. Just before we
got to Eaton, although I was never more thoroughly or
even excitedly awake in my life, I must have lost consciousness for a minute. I came to myself when the
coach was pulling up at an inn. I looked round instantly, and my companion was gone. I jumped out
on pretence of getting something to eat and drink, and

hastily asked the guard where the lady who had just got out was put into the coach. He said they had never stopped since they had last changed horses, and that I must have been dreaming. He knew nothing about the lady, and he looked at me suspiciously, as if he thought I was drunk. I for my part was perfectly confident that I had not been deluded by an apparition of my own brain. I had never suffered from ghost-like visitations of any kind, and my thoughts, owing to my preoccupation with business, had not run upon women in any way whatever. More convincing still, I had noticed that the lady wore a light blue neckerchief; and when I went back into the coach I found that she had left it behind her. I took it up, and I have it to this day. You may imagine how my mind dwelt upon that night. I got to Newcastle, did what I had to do, came back again, and made a point this time of sleeping at Eaton Socon in order to make inquiries. Everybody recollected the arrival of the down coach by which I travelled, and everybody was perfectly sure that no lady was in it. I produced the scarf, and asked whether anybody who lived near had been observed to wear it. Eaton is a little village, and all the people in it were as well known as if they belonged to one family, but nobody recognised it. It was certainly not English. I thought about the affair for months, partly because I was smitten with my visitor, and partly because I was half afraid my brain had been a little upset by worry. However, in time, the impression faded. Meanwhile I began to get on in the world, and after some three or four years my intense application was rewarded by riches. In seven or eight years I had become wealthy, and I began to think about settling myself in life. I had made the acquaintance of influential people in London, and more particularly of a certain baronet whom I had met in France while taking a holiday. Although I was in business I came of good family, and our acquaintance grew into something more. He had two or three daughters, to each of whom he was able to give a good marriage portion, and I became engaged to one of them. I don't know that there was much enthusiasm about our courtship. She was a very pleasant, good-looking girl, and although I can acquit myself of all mercenary motives in proposing to her, I cannot say that the highest motives were operative. I was as thousands of others are. I had got weary of loneliness; I wanted a home. I cast about me to see who amongst all the women I knew would best make me a wife. I selected this one, and perhaps the thought of her money may have been a trifle determinatory. I was not overmastered by a passion which I could not resist, nor was I coldly indifferent. If I had married her we should probably have lived a life of customary married comfort, and even of happiness; the same level, and perhaps slightly grey life which is lived by the ordinary English husband and wife. Things had gone so far that it was settled we were to be married in the spring of 1826, and I had begun to look out for a house, and make purchases in anticipation of housekeeping. In 1825 I had to go to Bristol. I shall never forget to the day of my death one morning in that city. I had had my breakfast, and was going out to see the head of one of the largest firms in the city, with whom I had an appointment. I met him in the street, and I noted before he spoke that there was something the matter. I soon found out what it was. The panic of 1825 had begun; three great houses in London had failed, and brought him down. He was a ruined man, and so was I. I managed to stagger back to the hotel, and found letters there confirming all that he had said. For some two or three days I was utterly prostrate, and could not summon sufficient strength to leave Bristol. One of the first things I did when I came to myself was to write to the baronet, telling him what had happened, that I was altogether penniless, and that in honour I felt bound to release his daughter from her engagement. I had a sympathising letter from him in return, saying that he was greatly afflicted at my misfortune, that his daughter was nearly broken-hearted, but that she had come to the conclusion that perhaps it would be best to accept my very kind offer. Much as she loved me, she felt that her health was far from strong, and although he had always meant to endow her generously on her marriage, her fortune alone would not enable her to procure those luxuries which, for her delicate constitution, alas! were necessaries. But the main reason with her was that she was sure that, with my independence, I should be unhappy if I felt that my wife's property was my support. His letter was long, but although much wrapped up, this was the gist of it. I went back to London, sold every stick I had, and tried to get a situation as clerk in some house, doing the business in which I had been engaged. I failed, for the distress was great, and I was reduced nearly to my last sovereign when I determined to go down to Newcastle, and try the friend there whom I had not seen since 1817. It was once more winter, and, although I was so poor, I was obliged to ride inside the coach again, for I was much troubled with my ancient enemy—the weakness in the chest. The incidents of my former visit I had nearly forgotten till we came near to Eaton Socon, and then they returned to me. But now it was a dull January day, with a bitter thaw, and my fellow passengers were a Lincolnshire squire, with his red-faced wife, who never spoke a syllable to me, and by reason of their isolation seemed to make the thaw all the more bitter, the fen levels all the more dismally flat, and the sky all the more leaden. At last we came to Newcastle. During the latter part of the journey I was alone, my Lincolnshire squire and his lady having left me on the road. It was about seven o'clock in the evening when we arrived; a miserable night, with the snow just melting under foot, and the town was wrapped in smoke and fog. I was so depressed that I hardly cared what became of me, and when I stepped out of the coach wished that I had been content to lie down and die in London. I could not put up at the coaching hotel, as it was too expensive, but walked on to one which was cheaper. I almost lost my way, and had wandered down a narrow street, which at every step became more and more squalid, and at last ended opposite a factory gate. Hard by was a wretched marine store shop, in the window of which were old iron, old teapots, a few old Bibles, and other miscellaneous effects. I stepped in to ask for directions to the Cross Keys. Coming out, whom should I see crossing the road, as if to meet me, but the

very lady who rode with me in the coach to Eaton some
nine years ago. There was no mistaking her. She seemed
scarcely a day older. The face was as lovely and as
inspired as ever. I was almost beside myself. I leaned
against the railing of the shop, and the light from the
window shone full on her. She came straight towards
me on to the pavement; looked at me, and turned up
the street. I followed her till we got to the end, determined not to lose sight of her; and we reached an open,
broad thoroughfare. She stopped at a bookseller's, and
went in. I was not more than two minutes after her; but
when I entered she was not there. A shopman was at
the counter, and I asked him whether a lady, my sister,
had not just left the shop. No lady, he said, had been
there for half-an-hour. I went back to the marine store
shop. The footsteps were still there which I saw her
make as she crossed. I knelt down, tracing them with
my fingers to make sure I was not deceived by my eyes,
and was more than ever confounded. At last I got to my
inn, and went to bed a prey to the strangest thoughts.
In the morning I was a little better. The stagnant blood
had been stirred by the encounter of the night before,
and though I was much agitated, and uncertain whether
my brain was actually sound or not, I was sufficiently
self-possessed and sensible to call upon my friend and
explain my errand. He did what he could to help me,
and I became his clerk in Newcastle. For a time I was
completely broken, but gradually I began to recover
my health and spirits a little. I had little or no responsibility, and nothing to absorb me after office hours. As a
relief and an occupation, I tried to take up with a science,

and chose geology. On Sundays I used to make long rambling excursions, and for a while I was pleased with my new toy. But by degrees it became less and less interesting. I suppose I had no real love for it. Furthermore, I had no opportunities for expression. My sorrow had secluded me. I demanded more from those around me than I had any right to expect. As a rule, we all of us demand from the world more than we are justified in demanding, especially if we suffer; and because the world is not so constituted that it can respond to us as eagerly and as sympathetically as we respond to ourselves, we become morose. So it was with me. People were sorry for me; but I knew that my trouble did not disturb them deeply, that when they left me, their faces, which were forcibly contracted while in my presence, instantly expanded into their ordinary self-satisfaction, and that if I were to die I should be forgotten a week after the funeral. I therefore recoiled from men, and frequently, with criminal carelessness and prodigality, rejected many an offer of kindness, not because I did not need it, but because I wanted too much of it. My science, as I have said, was a failure. I cannot tell how it may be with some exceptionally heroic natures, but with me expression in some form or other, if the thing which should be expressed is to live, is an absolute necessity. I cannot read unless I have somebody to whom I can speak about my reading, and I lose almost all power of thinking if thought after thought remains with me. Expression is as indispensable to me as expiration of breath. Inspiration of the air is a necessity, but continued inspiration of air without expiration of the same

is an impossibility. The geology was neglected, and at
first I thought it was because it was geology, and I tried
something else. For some months I fancied I had found
a solace in chemistry. With my savings I purchased
some apparatus, and began to be proficient. But the
charm faded from this also; the apparatus was put aside,
and the sight of it lying disused only made my dissatis-
faction and melancholy the more profound. Amidst all
my loneliness, I had never felt the least inclination to
any baser pleasures, nor had I ever seen a woman for
whom I felt even the most transient passion. My spec-
tral friend—if spectre she was—dominated my existence,
and seemed to prevent not only all licentiousness, but
all pleasure, except of the most superficial kind, in other
types of beauty. This need be no surprise to anybody.
I have known cases in which the face of a singularly
lovely woman, seen only for a few moments in the street,
has haunted a man all through his life, and deeply
affected it. In time I was advanced in my position as
clerk, and would have married, but I had not the least
inclination thereto. I did not believe in the actual reality
of my vision, and had no hope of ever meeting in the
flesh the apparition of the coach and the dingy street;
I felt sure that there was some mistake, something wrong
with me—the probabilities were all in favour of my
being deceived; but still the dream possessed me, and
every woman who for a moment appealed to me was
tried by that standard and found wanting.

'After some years had passed, during which I had
scarcely been out of Newcastle, I took a holiday, and
went up to London. It was about July. I was now a

man on the wrong side of fifty, shy, reserved, with a reputation for constitutional melancholy, a shadowy creature, of whom nobody took much notice and who was noticed by nobody. While in London I went to see the pictures at the Academy.* The place was thronged, and I was tired; I just looked about me, and was on the point of coming out wearied, when in a side room where there were crayon drawings, I caught sight of one of a face. I was amazed beyond measure. It was the face which had been my companion for so many years. There could be no mistake about it; even the necker-chief was tied as I remembered it so well, the very counterpart of the treasure I still preserved so sacredly at home. I was almost overcome with a faintness, with a creeping sensation all over the head, as if something were giving way, and with a shock of giddiness. I went and got a catalogue, found out the name of the artist, and saw that the picture had merely the name of "Stella" affixed to it. It might be a portrait, or it might not. After gazing myself almost blind at it, I went out and instantly posted to the artist's house. He was at home. He seemed a poor man, and was evidently surprised at any inquiry after his picture so late in the season. I asked him who sat for it. "Nobody," he said; "it was a mere fancy sketch. There might be a reminiscence in it of a girl I knew in France years ago; but she is long since dead, and I don't think that anybody who knew her would recognise a likeness in it. In fact, I am sure they would not." The price of the drawing was not much, although it was a good deal for me. I said instantly I would have it, and managed to get the money together by scraping up all my savings out of the savings bank. That is the very picture which you now see before you. I do not pretend to explain everything which I have told you. I have long since given up the attempt, and I suppose it must be said that I have suffered from some passing disorder of the brain, although that theory is not sound at all points, and there are circumstances inconsistent with it.'

The next morning my friend went to his office, after an early breakfast. His hours were long, and I was obliged to leave Newcastle before his return. So I bade him good-bye before he left home. I never saw him again. Two years afterwards I was shocked to see an announcement in the *Times* of his death. Knowing his lonely way of life, I went down to Newcastle to gather what I could about his illness and last moments. He had caught cold, and died of congestion of the lungs. His landlady said that he had made a will, and that what little property had remained after paying his funeral expenses had been made over to a hospital. I was anxious to know where the picture was. She could not tell me. It had disappeared just before his death, and nobody knew what had become of it.

EXPLANATORY NOTES

THE AUTOBIOGRAPHY OF MARK RUTHERFORD

xxxvi . . . *portion in life*: paraphrase of Ecclesiastes 9: 7–9.

2 *Liverpool and Manchester Railway*: the railway was opened on 15 September 1830.

small country town: White was born in Bedford on 22 December 1831.

4 *Eton Latin Grammar*: '. . . Latin in the lower school [at Bedford]—Greek was not taught—consisted almost entirely in learning the Eton Latin grammar by heart, and construing Cornelius Nepos' (*The Early Life of Mark Rutherford*, pp. 47–8).

A river ran through the town: the Ouse passes through the centre of Bedford.

5 *on the Sundays*: White invoked similar memories in *The Early Life of Mark Rutherford* (pp. 45–6): 'The recollections of boyhood, so far as week-days go, are very happy. Sunday, however, was not happy. I was taken to a religious service, morning and evening, and understood nothing. The evening was particularly trying. The windows of the meeting-house streamed inside with condensed breath, and the air we took into our lungs was poisonous. Almost every Sunday some woman was carried out fainting. Do what I could it was impossible to keep awake. When I was quite little I was made to stand on the seat, a spectacle, with other children in the like case, to the whole congregation, and I often nearly fell down, overcome with drowsiness.'

Calvinistic Independents: the religious body now known as the Congregationalists had its roots in the anticlerical soil of sixteenth-century Protestantism, and though it shared with Presbyterianism a high regard for the teachings of

John Calvin (1509–64), the French reformer and theologian, the English Independents were less fervently Calvinistic than the Scottish Presbyterians. 'Dissent had been strong throughout the whole county [of Bedfordshire] ever since the Commonwealth,' White recalled in *The Early Life of Mark Rutherford* (pp. 16–17). 'The old meeting-house held about 700 people, and was filled every Sunday. . . . Most of the well-to-do trades-folk were Dissenters. They were taught what was called a "moderate Calvinism", a phrase not easy to understand. If it had any meaning, it was that predestination, election, and reprobation, were unquestionably true, but they were dogmas about which it was not prudent to say much, for some of the congregation were a little Arminian, and St James could not be totally neglected.' (Arminians, unlike Calvinists, believed that God's grace was freely available to all sinners, and the Epistle of St James was distrusted by more orthodox Protestants because of its emphasis on good works rather than faith.)

Evangelical Magazine: published in London between 1793 and 1904.

6 *the chapel*: the meeting-house in Bedford that White frequented as a boy was known as the Old Meeting, a name later changed to the Bunyan Meeting because of the building's historic connection with John Bunyan.

singing pew: this reflects an arrangement sometimes found also in Anglican churches of the eighteenth and early nineteenth centuries, when the musicians generally sat in a gallery or singing-loft at the west end (memorably described in Hardy's *Under the Greenwood Tree*, 1872) or occasionally in a singing pew at the side or back of the nave. White offered a more detailed picture in *The Early Life of Mark Rutherford* (pp. 17–18): 'In the "singing-pew" sat a clarionet, a double bass, a bassoon, and a flute: also a tenor voice which "set the tune". The carpenter, to whom the tenor voice belonged, had a tuning-fork which he struck on his desk and applied to his ear. He then hummed the tuning-fork note, and the octave below, the double bass screwed up and responded, the leader with the tuning-fork struck out, everybody following, including the orchestra, and those of the congregation who had bass or tenor voices sang the air. Each of the instruments demanded a fair share of solos.'

12 *I had no experience to give*: 'I had to tell the church that my experience had not been eventful. I was young, and had enjoyed the privilege of godly parents' (*The Early Life of Mark Rutherford*, p. 58).

14 *a Dissenting College*: '. . . I was handed over to a private tutor to prepare for the Countess of Huntingdon's College at Cheshunt, which admitted students other than those which belonged to the Connexion, provided their creed did not materially differ from that which governed the Connexion trusts' (*The Early Life of Mark Rutherford*, p. 56). The College was in fact Anglican but associated with the extreme Evangelical wing of the Church.

16 *German literature*: from the eighteenth century onwards the German universities were the chief centres of the critical analysis of the authorship, sources, and textual accuracy of the Bible (i.e. what later came to be called 'the Higher Criticism'); hence in England, until surprisingly late in the Victorian period, the word 'German' suggested unimaginable heresies to most Christian believers. (See also Rutherford's reference to a 'German Gospel' on p. 93.)

21 *Damascus*: St Paul's conversion to Christianity, which took place when he was struck down by a blinding light while travelling to Damascus, is described in the ninth chapter of the Acts of the Apostles.

Lyrical Ballads: *Lyrical Ballads, with a Few Other Poems* by Wordsworth and Coleridge was published in 1798. White said later that he remembered 'as a lad first coming on a volume of Wordsworth. He *came on* it; it was not thrust upon him' (*Groombridge Diary*, p. 33).

26 *Union meeting*: the annual meeting of the Independent churches (now known as the Congregational Union of England and Wales).

29 *just and unjust alike*: '. . . for he [God] maketh the sun to rise on the evil and the good, and sendeth rain on the just and on the unjust' (Matthew 5: 45).

32 *Bell's Weekly Messenger*: the full title was *Bell's New Weekly Messenger*; published in London between 1832 and 1855.

35 *'serious'*: a word that by the beginning of the nineteenth century, among English Evangelicals and Nonconformists, had acquired the meaning of religiously devout.

36 *Vicar of Wakefield*: Snale may object to Oliver Goldsmith's novel (1776) because of a lingering distrust of fiction in Nonconformist circles.

George Fox's Journal: the *Journal* (1694) of George Fox (1624–91), founder of the Society of Friends, was regarded as one of the classics of Nonconformist devotional literature.

39 *Cowper*: Rutherford's indifference to William Cowper (1731–1800), the celebrated evangelical poet, is surprising, particularly since many of Cowper's best-known hymns were composed in Olney, a village in Buckinghamshire not very distant from Bedford.

43 *the Valley of the Shadow*: 'Yea, though I walk through the valley of the shadow of death, I will fear no evil' (Psalm 23: 4). Bunyan's Christian also passes through the Valley of the Shadow of Death in *The Pilgrim's Progress*.

48 *the true Paschal Lamb*: Christians have interpreted the Paschal lamb, sacrificed and eaten by the Israelites at Passover, as a symbol of Christ.

Westminster Confession: a Presbyterian creed drawn up in England during the seventeenth century.

49 *Balaam*: the narrative of Balaam appears in Numbers, chapters 22–4, and is mentioned elsewhere in the Bible. White remarked to his future second wife in 1908 that 'of

all the stories in the Bible, the story of Balaam's ass was the one he should least like to lose, and he wished there were many more such asses' (*The Groombridge Diary*, pp. 3–4).

51 *pure and unspotted*: 'Pure religion and undefiled before God and the Father is this, To visit the fatherless and widows in their affliction, and to keep himself unspotted from the world' (James 1: 27).

52 *Edward Gibbon Mardon*: Mardon is named after the historian Edward Gibbon (1737–94), whose name had become a byword for scepticism because of his hostile treatment of the Christian church in *The Decline and Fall of the Roman Empire* (1776–88). Basil Willey (*More Nineteenth Century Studies*, p. 212) describes Mardon as 'a type of the devout "unbeliever" of the nineteenth century, [who embodies] some traits of men like Francis Newman, Frederic Harrison, Leslie Stephen, W. R. Greg, T. H. Huxley . . .'.

55 *that awful Friday afternoon*: Jesus was crucified on Friday and died, according to tradition, in mid-afternoon.

57 *Windsor chairs*: a type of wooden chair originally manufactured in Berkshire.

64 *conformation*: 'the manner in which a thing is formed with respect to the disposition of its parts' (*OED*).

75 *lines of Cowper*: Cowper's 'Charity' (1782), lines 435–40.

82 *Enemy of Souls*: Satan.

83 *Vesuvian*: of volcanic violence or power; after Vesuvius, the active volcano on the Bay of Naples.

86 *Unitarian*: Rutherford seems to be using the term here in a generic sense of one who believes in God but rejects the divinity of Christ; he is not referring to Unitarianism as a religious body (for which see the note below for p. 109).

92 "*. . . jewels in the sky*": The hymn misquoted by Snale is apparently an adaptation of Psalm 19.

93 *Rock of Ages*: Christian commentators have often regarded
the rock struck by Moses with a rod (Numbers 20: 11) as a
symbolic representation of Christ, but the specific reference here is to Augustus Toplady's 'Rock of Ages', which
was perhaps the most popular hymn among Evangelicals
and Dissenters in nineteenth-century England.

107 *despised*: Handel's libretto is based at this point on a
Messianic prophecy in the Old Testament: 'He was
despised and rejected of men; a man of sorrows, and
acquainted with grief' (Isaiah 53: 3).

109 *Unitarian*: Unitarianism, which rejects the orthodox
Christian teaching of a Deity consisting of three Persons
(God the Father, Christ, and the Holy Spirit), developed
variously in several European countries, but in England
and Scotland during the late eighteenth century it
flourished among Dissenting—especially Presbyterian—
congregations. White comments again on this historical
development on p. 118.

115 *loadstone*: magnet.

118 *Wesleyans*: Methodism, founded by John Wesley (1703–
91), was originally a reforming movement within the
Church of England but split off as a separate denomina-
tion after his death. In time there were several Methodist
bodies in England, and of these the Wesleyan Methodists
remained the closest in liturgy and doctrine to the Church
of England. In a letter written in July 1899 (*Letters to Three
Friends*, pp. 93–4), White observed: 'Wesley was, so I have
always thought, a really great man. He had true religious
insight, he was self-denying as any apostle or mediaeval
saint, giving all his goods to feed the poor, and he had a
genius, almost Napoleonic, for command; but he was born
in a bad time when the proper development of such gifts
as his was impossible. Caught up into the strange
eighteenth-century element of ecclesiastical lying, and,
struggling against it, he emerged imperfect as we behold
him.'

123 *butterfly net*: 'The "butterfly collector" ... is almost certainly a portrait of Selwyn Image [artist and amateur entomologist, 1849–1930]' (Wilfred H. Stone, *Religion and Art of William Hale White (Mark Rutherford)*, p. 129 n.).

132 *Stoke Newington*: when Edgar Allan Poe lived in Stoke Newington—on the northern edge of London, near Highbury—in 1820, it had a population of 2,000, and he described it as 'a misty looking village'; but by 1864 another writer reported that 'all around the builders are drawing a close cordon of bricks' (Nikolaus Pevsner, *London except the Cities of London and Westminster* (The Buildings of England, 1952), p. 427). White accepted a position as a schoolmaster in Stoke Newington in the autumn of 1852 but abandoned it within twenty-four hours; the account he offers of the episode in *The Early Life of Mark Rutherford* (pp. 79–81) is virtually identical to the passage that follows in the *Autobiography*.

139 *'delivered me!'*: see note above for p. 43.

Paternoster Row: a street near St Paul's Cathedral that was for several centuries the centre of the English bookselling and publishing trade.

141 *a publisher ... who published and sold books of a sceptical turn*:'I called on several publishers and asked for employment, but could get none till I came to John Chapman, editor and proprietor of the *Westminster Review*, as well as publisher, mainly of books which were theologically heretical, and, I am sorry to say, did not pay. He lived at 142 Strand' (*The Early Life of Mark Rutherford*, p. 82). Chapman (1822–94) became the editor and proprietor of the *Westminster Review* in 1851.

143 *'niece Theresa'*: Theresa is a fictionalized portrait of George Eliot, who resided with Chapman for two years while acting as sub-editor of the *Westminster Review*. 'It is a lasting sorrow to me that I allowed my friendship with her to drop,' White wrote late in life, 'and that after I left Chapman I never called on her. . . . I knew that she was

not only endowed with extraordinary genius, but with human qualities even more precious' (*The Early Life of Mark Rutherford*, pp. 83–4).

146 *holy of holies*: the most sacred portion of the Israelite tabernacle (and later the Temple in Jerusalem) contained the Ark of the Covenant and was thought to be especially blessed by God's presence; only the High Priest was allowed to enter it once a year. The phrase used in the Authorized Version to describe it is 'most holy place' (Exodus 26: 34), but Wyclif rendered it as 'holy of holies' in his translation, and by the nineteenth century the latter phrase was often used metaphorically to describe some inner recess of the human mind or heart.

152 *The Lass of Lochroyan*: White quotes the version of the ballad supplied by Sir Walter Scott in *Minstrelsy of the Scottish Border* (1802).

153 *chief failings*: White's unflattering self-portrait here is misleading, since he was offered a partnership at Chapman's (which he declined).

155 *'demy octavo . . . twelvemo'*: two standard formats of books: the demy octavo page was 8½ x 5½ inches, the twelvemo (or duodecimo) somewhat smaller.

157 *beatitude*: the beatitudes (a word that does not appear in the Bible) were delivered by Christ in his Sermon on the Mount (Matthew, chapters 5–7).

163 *Thus far*: the final words in the novel are given to Rutherford's fictional editor, Reuben Shapcott.

NOTES ON THE BOOK OF JOB

Mark Rutherford's Deliverance (2nd edition, pp. 272–3) concludes with these words by Reuben Shapcott: 'On looking over his papers, I found the sketch of his life and a mass of odds and ends, some apparently written for publication. Many of these had evidently been in books, and had most likely, therefore, been offered to editors or publishers, but all, I am sure, had been refused. I add one or two by way of appendix, and hope they will be thought worth saving.' 'Notes on the Book of Job' and 'Principles' then followed in the first edition of the *Deliverance*; 'A Mysterious Portrait' was added in the second edition (1888) of both the *Autobiography* and *Deliverance*. The thematic connection between the life of Mark Rutherford and the Old Testament figure of Job is evident: both are God-obsessed men who suffer greatly when compelled by circumstances to call into question the moral purpose of the universe.

170 *sphinx-like*: silent and mysterious.

171 *There the wicked . . . at rest*: Job 3: 17.

174 *Age after age . . . perfect man*: paraphrase of Job 8: 16, 8: 20.

175 *Arcturus, Orion, and the Pleiades:* stars and constellations.

   Vulgate: the Latin version of the Bible compiled by St Jerome in the fourth century.

183 *Uz*: the native place of Job, traditionally associated with Edom.

188 *Ophir*: a place mentioned twelve times in the Old Testament, usually in connection with precious stones; its actual location is a subject of conjecture.

189 *covet fields . . . his heritage*: Micah 2: 2.

190 *philological evidence*: some Biblical scholars have regarded the speeches of Elihu (chapters 32–7) as a later interpolation.

192 *behemoth and the leviathan*: it is usually assumed that these Biblical names refer to the hippopotamus and crocodile respectively.

194 *patience*: 'In your patience possess ye your souls' (Luke 21: 19).

PRINCIPLES

197 *Moses*: the leader of the Israelites who delivered them out of their Egyptian bondage is cited here because he was known as the Lawgiver.

200 *Alpha and Omega*: the first and last letters in the Greek alphabet—i.e. the beginning and end (of life).

Canaanites: the original pagan inhabitants of Palestine.

clean beasts and unclean beasts: the Mosaic code made a clear distinction between ritually clean and unclean animals, the latter of which were not to be touched or eaten by the Israelites.

201 *Sirens*: the sea nymphs who tempted mariners to their death by singing on an island surrounded by treacherous rocks. Ulysses resisted their lure by having himself strapped to a mast.

Penelope: Ulysses' wife.

203 *carle hemp*: Scottish proverbial expression for great strength; literally, the seed-bearing hemp plant. 'Come, *Firm Resolve* take thou the van, / Thou stalk o' carl-hemp in man!' (Burns, 'To Dr. Blacklock', lines 43–4).

204 *Epaminondas . . . Lycurgus . . . Agesilaus*: three figures of Greek antiquity—general of Thebes, founder of the Spartan constitution, and king of Sparta respectively.

Idaei Dactyli: a mythical body of men associated with Mount Ida in Phrygia.

A MYSTERIOUS PORTRAIT

This story was first published anonymously in the *Birmingham Daily Post* on 24 December 1881.

208 *Eaton Socon*:a market town north-east of Bedford.

216 *the Academy*: The Royal Academy.

THE WORLD'S CLASSICS

A Select List

SERGEI AKSAKOV: A Russian Gentleman
Translated by J. D. Duff
Edited by Edward Crankshaw

HANS ANDERSEN: Fairy Tales
Translated by L. W. Kingsland
Introduction by Naomi Lewis
Illustrated by Vilhelm Pedersen and Lorenz Frølich

ARTHUR J. ARBERRY (Transl.): The Koran

LUDOVICO ARIOSTO: Orlando Furioso
Translated by Guido Waldman

ARISTOTLE: The Nicomachean Ethics
Translated by David Ross

JANE AUSTEN: Emma
Edited by James Kinsley and David Lodge

Northanger Abbey, Lady Susan, The Watsons,
and **Sanditon**
Edited by John Davie

Persuasion
Edited by John Davie

ROBERT BAGE: Hermsprong
Edited by Peter Faulkner

WILLIAM BECKFORD: Vathek
Edited by Roger Lonsdale

KEITH BOSLEY (Transl.): The Kalevala

CHARLOTTE BRONTË: Jane Eyre
Edited by Margaret Smith

JOHN BUNYAN: The Pilgrim's Progress
Edited by N. H. Keeble

FRANCES HODGSON BURNETT: The Secret Garden
Edited by Dennis Butts

The Two Drovers and Other Stories
Edited by Graham Tulloch
Introduction by Lord David Cecil

SIR PHILIP SIDNEY:
The Countess of Pembroke's Arcadia (The Old Arcadia)
Edited by Katherine Duncan-Jones

TOBIAS SMOLLETT: The Expedition of Humphry Clinker
Edited by Lewis M. Knapp
Revised by Paul-Gabriel Boucé

ROBERT LOUIS STEVENSON: Treasure Island
Edited by Emma Letley

ANTHONY TROLLOPE: The American Senator
Edited by John Halperin